D0463555

YOUNG ADULT

DA   958.104 $22.95
      AFG   Afghanistan

                 Jefferson Township Public Lib

                         ONLINE

MORRIS AUTOMATED INFORMATION NETWORK

0 1014 0124145 6

MAY --   2005

WITHDRAWN

Jefferson Twp. Public Library
      1031 Weldon Road
    Oak Ridge, NJ 07438
      (973) 208-6115

THE WORLD'S H🔥T SPOTS

Afghanistan

THE WORLD'S H🔥T SPOTS

Afghanistan

John Boaz, *Book Editor*

Jefferson Twp. Public Library
1031 Weldon Road
Oak Ridge, NJ 07438
(973) 208-6115

Daniel Leone, *President*
Bonnie Szumski, *Publisher*
Scott Barbour, *Managing Editor*

GREENHAVEN
PRESS ®

THOMSON
™
GALE

San Diego • Detroit • New York • San Francisco • Cleveland
New Haven, Conn. • Waterville, Maine • London • Munich

© 2004 by Greenhaven Press. Greenhaven Press is an imprint of The Gale Group, Inc.,
a division of Thomson Learning, Inc.

Greenhaven® and Thomson Learning™ are trademarks used herein under license.

For more information, contact
Greenhaven Press
27500 Drake Rd.
Farmington Hills, MI 48331-3535
Or you can visit our Internet site at http://www.gale.com

ALL RIGHTS RESERVED.
No part of this work covered by the copyright hereon may be reproduced or used in any form
or by any means—graphic, electronic, or mechanical, including photocopying, recording,
taping, Web distribution or information storage retrieval systems—without the written
permission of the publisher.

Every effort has been made to trace the owners of copyrighted material.

Cover credit: © AP/Wide World Photos

LIBRARY OF CONGRESS CATALOGING-IN-PUBLICATION DATA

Afghanistan / John Boaz, book editor.
  p. cm. — (The world's hot spots)
Includes bibliographical references and index.
ISBN 0-7377-1722-X (pbk. : alk. paper) — ISBN 0-7377-1721-1 (lib. : alk. paper)
  1. Afghanistan—History—Soviet occupation, 1979–1989. 2. Afghanistan—
History—1989–2001. 3. Afghanistan—History—2001– . I. Boaz, John. II. Series.
DS371.2.A3384 2004
958.104'5—dc21
                                                                    2003044856

Printed in the United States of America

⚝ CONTENTS

Chapter 1: A Turbulent History

1. Afghanistan's Troubled History

In response to a lack of U.S. support in the early years
of the Cold War, Afghanistan became dependent on the
Soviet Union for developmental assistance. This development hastened the country's fall into chaos in the
1980s and 1990s.

2. The Soviet Invasion and the Rise of Islamic Terrorism

The Soviet Union's 1979 invasion of Afghanistan and the
subsequent civil war set the stage for the establishment
and growth of the al-Qaeda terrorist network. As a result,
Afghanistan became a base for terrorism worldwide.

3. The Rise of the Taliban

The Taliban, a fundamentalist Muslim faction, gained
control of most of Afghanistan between 1994 and 1996.
The regime imposed repressive restrictions, but also provided an alternative to the bitter fighting that had ravaged Afghanistan for several years.

4. The U.S.-Led Attack on Afghanistan and the Fall of the Taliban

On October 7, 2001, a U.S.-led international force began
bombing targets in Afghanistan in an effort to disrupt the
activities of the al-Qaeda terrorist network and depose
their Taliban hosts. This was the first major military assault in the war on terror, and within just a few weeks it
resulted in the fall of the Taliban.

Chapter 2: Post-Taliban Afghanistan: Reconstruction and Nation Building

Central Asian affairs, which in turn could undermine the stability it seeks to create.

♦ FOREWORD

T he American Heritage Dictionary defines the term *hot spot* as "an area in which there is dangerous unrest or hostile action." Though it is probably true that almost any conceivable "area" contains potentially "dangerous unrest or hostile action," there are certain countries in the world especially susceptible to conflict that threatens the lives of noncombatants on a regular basis. After the events of September 11, 2001, the consequences of this particular kind of conflict and the importance of the countries, regions, or groups that produce it are even more relevant for all concerned public policy makers, citizens, and students. Perhaps now more than ever, the violence and instability that engulfs the world's hot spots truly has a global reach and demands the attention of the entire international community.

The scope of problems caused by regional conflicts is evident in the extent to which international policy makers have begun to assert themselves in efforts to reduce the tension and violence that threatens innocent lives around the globe. The U.S. Congress, for example, recently addressed the issue of economic stability in Pakistan by considering a trading bill to encourage growth in the Pakistani textile industry. The efforts of some congresspeople to improve the economic conditions in Pakistan through trade with the United States was more than an effort to address a potential economic cause of the instability engulfing Pakistani society. It was also an acknowledgment that domestic issues in Pakistan are connected to domestic political issues in the United States. Without a concerted effort by policy makers in the United States, or any other country for that matter, it is quite possible that the violence and instability that shatters the lives of Pakistanis will not only continue, but will also worsen and threaten the stability and prosperity of other regions.

Recent international efforts to reach a peaceful settlement of the Israeli-Palestinian conflict also demonstrate how peace and stability in the Middle East is not just a regional issue. The toll on Palestinian and Israeli lives is easy to see through the suicide bombings and rocket attacks in Israeli cities and in the occupied territories of the West Bank and Gaza. What is, perhaps, not as evident is the extent to which this conflict involves the rest of the world. Saudi Arabia and Iran, for instance, have long been at odds and have attempted to gain control of the conflict by supporting competing organizations dedicated to a Palestinian state. These groups have often used Saudi and Iranian financial and political support to carry out violent attacks against Israeli civilians and military installations. Of course, the issue goes far beyond a struggle between two regional powers to gain control of the region's most visible issue. Many analysts and leaders have also argued that the West's military and political support of Israel is one of the leading factors that motivated al-Qaeda's September 11 attacks on New York and Washington, D.C. In many ways, this regional conflict is an international affair that will require international solutions.

The World's Hot Spots series is intended to meet the demand for information and discussion among young adults and students who would like to better understand the areas embroiled in conflicts that contribute to catastrophic events like those of September 11. Each volume of The World's Hot Spots is an anthology of primary and secondary documents that provides historical background to the conflict, or conflicts, under examination. The books also provide students with a wide range of opinions from world leaders, activists, and professional writers concerning the root causes and potential solutions to the problems facing the countries covered in this series. In addition, extensive research tools such as an annotated table of contents, bibliography, and glossaries of terms and important figures provide readers a foundation from which they can build their knowledge of some of the world's most pressing issues. The information and opinions presented in The World's Hot Spots series will give students some of the tools they will need to become active participants in the ongoing dialogue concerning the globe's most volatile regions.

♦ INTRODUCTION

On September 9, 2001, Ahmad Shah Massoud, the charismatic longtime leader of Afghanistan's Northern Alliance, which opposed the reigning Taliban regime, agreed to an interview with two Algerian journalists. The journalists were ushered into Massoud's compound for the interview. Nothing seemed to be out of the ordinary. During the interview, however, a bomb that had been concealed in the Algerians' camera exploded, killing the two "journalists" and mortally wounding Massoud. He died during the helicopter flight to a hospital in the neighboring country of Tajikistan.

The suicide attack on Massoud went virtually unreported by news agencies in Western nations. Afghanistan, a country subject to militant Islamic fundamentalist rule, has long been known for its brutal wars, tribal conflicts, and terrorist activity. The fact that the assassination had probably been orchestrated by Osama bin Laden's terrorist network al-Qaeda ("the base"), which the Taliban harbored, did not seem to be of any great importance. All of al-Qaeda's previous operations had occurred in Africa or Asia, so Western governments had no reason to fear that al-Qaeda might be expanding its terrorist activities or to see Massoud's death as anything other than business as usual in Central Asia. It seemed likely that the assassination was little more than the gesture of a thankful guest making use of his resources to rid his hosts of their chief enemy. Two days later, Massoud's assassination would be viewed in a completely different context, and Afghanistan would once again be in the forefront of world events.

Within ninety minutes on the morning of September 11, 2001, two hijacked commercial airliners struck the Twin Towers of the World Trade Center in New York City, a third jet slammed into the Pentagon, and a fourth jet crashed in rural Pennsylvania. It did not take long for news services and government intelligence agencies to realize that the United States was under attack. Millions of people around the world watched their television sets in horror as the Trade Center towers came crashing to the ground. It took less than a day for the U.S. government to identify most of the hijackers, all of whom had connections to bin Laden's al-Qaeda terrorist network. This made bin Laden a prime target, and Massoud's assassination now appeared to be the opening move in a much larger campaign. Whether Massoud's death satisfied a debt of gratitude for the Taliban's support of al-Qaeda or was a move to weaken anti-Taliban forces, the timing of the assassination could not be coincidence. Bin Laden had made his move in both Afghanistan and the West.

In response to the attacks on U.S. soil, the United States demanded justice. Going after bin Laden, however, meant either pressuring the Taliban to hand him over or launching a military strike against Afghanistan. When Mullah Omar, the leader of the Taliban, refused to hand over bin Laden, it was clear that military action would be necessary not only against bin Laden and al-Qaeda, but also against the Taliban regime that was harboring the terrorists.

This chain of events, from the assassination of Massoud to U.S. military action against the Taliban regime, is the latest phase in an ancient cycle of conflict and devastation in Afghanistan. The country has been and continues to be shaped by foreign invasions; civil, tribal, and ethnic conflict; and the influence of the Islamic fundamentalist movement.

Foreign Invasion and Civil Unrest

Afghanistan has always been a target of foreign invasions and has been subject to civil war and ethnic conflict throughout its history, with ruinous consequences for the Afghan nation and people. Though a landlocked and mostly desolate place, Afghanistan is the crossroads of Central Asia, an overland route that connects India, Russia, western Asia, and ultimately Europe. Alexander the Great, the Greek conqueror who forged an empire that stretched from the Mediterranean Sea to India, invaded and subdued the region as early as 330 B.C. Arab Muslims began to travel east of Iran, toward Afghanistan, in A.D. 637 and converted the people of the region to Islam. When they left, the Afghans developed dynasties and kingdoms of their own, until Genghis Khan and his vast nomadic army swept out of Mongolia in the east. Until the mid–eighteenth century, in fact, Afghanistan was subject to a series of foreign rulers and brief periods of rule by local tribal groups.

Beginning in roughly 1747, Afghanistan's political affairs fell under the domination of the Pashtun tribe. Pashtuns are the dominant ethnic group of Afghanistan, comprising about 38 percent of the population. Tajiks, Uzbeks, Hazaras, and other smaller groups make up the rest of the population. Though all are Muslim, each ethnic group has its own languages, origin, and traditions. The Pashtuns reside, for the most part, in the southern areas of Afghanistan along the Pakistani border, while the other groups are concentrated mostly in the north and center of the country. After centuries of fragmentation and exploitation by foreign powers, it was under the leadership of the first Pashtun ruler Ahmad Shah that Afghanistan began to take shape as a nation. He took control of the region through a series of daring military campaigns and, for the first time, Afghanistan was under the domination of a single local ruler. Within fifty years of Ahmad Shah's death, however, disputes over the legitimate heir to Shah's kingdom had plunged Afghanistan into civil war. The severity of the internal fighting following Ahmad Shah's death left Afghanistan vulnerable to the influence of the region's two great imperialist powers, Great Britain and Russia.

Britain had maintained a presence in India since about 1600, and by the mid–nineteenth century, the British Empire had expanded throughout the Indian subcontinent and the British government controlled Indian affairs. It was clear to the British that the greatest threat to their interests in India would come from Russia, Afghanistan's neighbor to the north. The Russians, likewise, viewed permanent British control in Central Asia as a direct threat to their empire. The struggle between England and Russia for dominance in Central Asia in the nineteenth century became known as the "Great Game." Both the British and the Russians saw Afghanistan as a buffer state, a divider, between their two empires. The power vacuum left by the ravages of the Afghan civil wars in the wake of Ahmad Shah's death led the British to suspect the Russians might use the region as an invasion route to India, a tactic that Alexander the Great had successfully employed. The British, consequently, invaded Afghanistan twice between 1838 and 1849 ostensibly to stabilize the region and to manage the country's foreign affairs. These invasions, known as the Anglo-Afghan Wars, in effect subjugated Afghanistan to British control and subordinated Afghanistan to the status of a buffer state between British-controlled India and Russia throughout the nineteenth and the early part of the twentieth century.

British interference in Afghan affairs was to have unintended consequences for Afghanistan, especially in regard to determining the exact borders of the country. The boundaries of Afghanistan tended to shift according to who was ruling the nation, how successfully a ruler was able to bring the tribes under his sway, or how aggressive Afghanistan's Russian and British neighbors were at any given time. The British fixed the boundary between India and Afghanistan in 1893. This border was known as the Durand Line, named after Sir Mortimer Durand, the British Indian foreign secretary who headed the mission to establish it. British dominance in India collapsed in the early twentieth century; however, the Great Game ended too, as did British control over Afghan affairs. Weakened by World War I and weary of colonial involvement the British relinquished control of Afghanistan, and Afghan independence officially became a reality in 1919. With independence came the difficulties of self-government, including political infighting and tribal uprisings, but it was the issue of the British-created Durand Line that most severely affected Afghan affairs for years to come in the form of border disputes with Pakistan.

Pakistan was created in 1947 when the British, exhausted by World War II and unable to suppress continual Indian uprisings, granted independence to India. The Muslim population of India's Northwest Frontier Province voted to form the Muslim nation of Pakistan, independent from a mostly Hindu India. Pakistan borders Afghanistan to the south along the Durand Line, which cuts through the traditional tribal lands of the nomadic Pashtuns. The issue of whether the Pashtun tribes should be absorbed into Afghanistan or Pakistan was never fully resolved, which led to cross-border skirmishes between Afghan Pashtuns and Pakistani forces. Pakistan responded to the deteriorating situation by halting most trade with Afghanistan in 1950, including all shipments of petroleum, and the Afghan economy suffered tremendously. The border clash with Pakistan and the subsequent cessation of trade forced Afghanistan to look to its northern neighbor, Russia, for help.

The government of Afghanistan signed a major agreement with the Soviets, and a new era of foreign interference began. All through the 1950s and 1960s, the Soviets provided economic and financial assistance to Afghanistan, and in return the Soviets were allowed to explore oil and natural gas reserves in the northern part of Afghanistan. They built military installations and airfields in Mazār-e-Sharīf and Bagram. The fact that the Soviets more than compensated for Afghanistan's lack of trade with Pakistan also meant that the "Pashtunistan issue," as the territorial dispute with Pakistan was known, was allowed to fester. Hostility continued; Pakistan and Afghanistan severed diplomatic relations in 1961 and all border traffic between the two countries came to a halt. Pakistan even closed its borders to the nomadic Pashtuns on the Afghan side of the border. Afghanistan became almost entirely dependent on trade with the Soviet Union, and the Soviets, in turn, expected an enormous return on their investment in Afghanistan.

The Soviet Invasion

The Soviet-Afghan relationship was shaky at best and, though the trade agreement heavily favored Soviet interests, Afghanistan's political instability made the Soviets fear that their investment in Afghanistan might come to nothing. By the 1960s, Soviet/Communist influence led to a new wave of civil unrest. The People's Democratic Party of Afghanistan (PDPA), a Communist organization, became politically active in the late 1960s. Originally formed as a cohesive unit by Nur Mohammad Taraki and Barbak Karmal, the PDPA split in 1967 into the Khalq (or Masses) faction under Taraki and the Parcham (or Banner) faction under Karmal. The split appeared to be along ideological lines, but was truly based on personality differences between the two men and the ethnic makeup of their respective constituencies. Supporters of the Khalq faction were overwhelmingly Pashtuns from the rural parts of the country, while the Parchamis were multiethnic and much more cosmopolitan.

From 1969 to 1973, instability became the norm in Afghan politics as external pressures and internal political struggles began to take their toll. A series of shifts in leadership occurred. In late 1973, the former prime minister of Afghanistan, Mohammad Daoud, seized power in a bloodless military coup while Afghanistan's king, Zahir Shah, was out of the country. In 1978 the PDPA seized power in a military coup and installed the leader of the Khalq faction, Taraki, as president. Although the PDPA was a Communist organization, political struggles within the party made the Russians nervous. Taraki's power was almost immediately challenged by his foreign minister, Hafizullah Amin, also a member of the Khalq faction. In October 1979, Amin had Taraki assassinated and became president. The Soviets, who had backed Taraki, were not at all pleased by Amin's maneuvers. Amin refused to take Soviet advice on how to stabilize the government, which the Soviets saw as an attempt to lessen Russian influence. The Soviets had invested considerable time and money nurturing trade and military associations with Afghanistan and, as Amin became more defiant toward Moscow, and popular internal resistance to Amin's rule increased, the Soviets began to fear that their huge investment in Afghanistan might be lost. Faced with a deteriorating security situation that threatened Soviet interests in Afghanistan, the Soviets launched an all-out invasion of the country on December 25, 1979.

The Soviet invasion was triggered, to a large extent, by the power struggle within the PDPA government, but two other main factors are thought to have been pivotal in the Soviet decision to invade. First, the Soviets feared having an unstable government so close to its southern borders. The second factor is known as the Brezhnev Doctrine, named after Leonid Brezhnev, leader of the Soviet Union from 1964 to 1982, which stated that the Soviet Union had a right to assist an endangered Socialist government. The Soviets believed that the fledgling Afghan Communist government could not survive the mounting internal resistance against it and that, therefore, intervention was necessary and justified. Whatever the reasons, the Soviet invasion had enormous consequences for Afghanistan.

International condemnation of the invasion was immediate and unequivocal, and Afghanistan became a focus of foreign interests. Several nations called for Soviet withdrawal. The United States saw an opportunity to weaken the Soviet Union, its Cold War rival, and to assist the embattled Afghan people. The United States could not engage in direct military conflict with the Soviet Union, however, because such action risked escalation into a global, perhaps even nuclear, war. Instead, the United States immediately channeled money to the Afghan mujahideen, or Islamic freedom fighters, who opposed the Soviets and the PDPA, via the Pakistani secret police, Inter-Services Intelligence (ISI). In this way, Pakistan once again became deeply involved in Afghan affairs. The United States offered Pakistan a generous military and economic assistance package in return, and many other nations offered aid in order to help Pakistan deal with the massive influx of Afghan refugees.

The cost of the war to both the Soviets and the Afghans is incalculable. Perhaps as many as 5 million Afghans fled to Pakistan, where many of them formed additional guerrilla units to strike Soviet targets in Afghanistan. The mujahideen were supplied with weapons by several nations, including the United States and Saudi Arabia, making the Afghan population one of the most heavily armed in the world, a problem that persists to this day. Much of the Afghan economy is based on agriculture, and the war left much farmland either incapable of bearing crops or heavily mined. The Soviet Union found itself paying a high price militarily within Afghanistan and in the souring of international relations with Western and Islamic countries alike. Unable to sustain the cost of prolonged military action and facing continued outcry for the end of the war from the Russian people and the international community, the Soviet army withdrew completely from Afghanistan by February 1989.

When the Soviets withdrew, the puppet regime left to rule in their place was unable to sustain its authority without the aid of the Soviet military. By 1992, the mujahideen finally entered the capital city of Kabul, and many voiced hopes that the years of war would finally come to an end. Instead, fighting broke out among the mujahideen factions themselves. They had been united loosely by their Islamic roots against the Soviet Union but, in the absence of their common enemy, their differences emerged, which resulted in civil war. Large-scale fighting was rampant in the northern areas and in Kabul. Afghanistan was left a wasteland subject to the whims of the tribal mujahideen warlords, who fought as bitterly with one another as they had fought the Soviet army. Not for the first time in Afghan history, foreign invasion and interference had given way to civil war. The country was on the verge of total anarchy. The years of unbroken conflict gave rise to a new wave of militant Islam that seemed, for a time, to bring hope to a ravaged, divided Afghanistan. Instead, fundamentalist, militant Islam in Afghanistan brought destruction to New York City, Washington, D.C., and Pennsylvania.

The Evolving Role of Islam

Islam has been a central, pervasive influence throughout Afghan society since it was brought to the region in A.D. 637. By providing a comprehensive code of social behavior regulating all human relationships, Islam has always been the most powerful common denominator among Afghanistan's various tribes and ethnicities. The doctrine was first applied to state building in the late nineteenth century by the Afghan leader Amir Abdur Rahman in an attempt to centralize government power. By relying on Islam as the basis for law and authority, the state had an instrument for ruling Afghanistan that cut across ethnic and tribal lines. The recent invasions and civil wars in Afghanistan, however, have allowed fundamentalist extremists to manipulate Islam and dominate Afghan society and politics.

When the Soviets invaded in 1979, it was Islam that brought the mujahideen resistance together. With the breakdown of the mujahideen alliance into civil war, Islam served to unite what became one of the most oppressive ruling regimes in Afghanistan's history: the Taliban, which derives its name from the Arabic word *talib*, meaning "pupil" or "seeker of knowledge." Most Taliban constituents were of Pashtun descent, and the Pashtuns had been the dominant ethnic group in Afghan affairs for centuries. The lack of order in Afghanistan in general—created by the infighting among the mujahideen—combined with a lack of Pashtun representation in the mujahideen government (which had been mostly Tajik) led to the emergence of the Taliban. Led by Mullah Omar, the Taliban leadership emerged first in the mostly Pashtun southern city of Kandahar. From there it spread through the rest of the country fairly quickly with support from Pakistan. By 1996 the Taliban had captured Kabul, and the remaining mujahideen forces fled to the northern provinces to form the anti-Taliban United Front, more popularly known as the Northern Alliance, while the Taliban consolidated their power.

The Taliban's stated goals were to restore order to a war-ravaged country by removing the warring mujahideen commanders, or warlords, and by imposing Islamic law in Afghan society. The Afghan people, exhausted and demoralized from decades of endless conflict, were willing to accept Taliban rule at first. As time went on, it became clear that the Taliban intended to impose an extreme interpretation of Islam on the nation. The regime's oppression of the Afghan people was no improvement over the violence that had been the norm under mujahideen rule. The Taliban perpetrated many human rights violations, mostly directed at women. Women were not permitted to work outside the home or to travel in public without a male escort. They were forced to wear a head-to-toe veil, known as a *burka*. Music was banned, as were artistic representations of humans or animals. Men were forced to grow beards, wear turbans, and pray five times daily, preferably in a mosque.

The Taliban's extremism attracted like-minded Islamic militants and their organizations, which the regime harbored in turn. Several fundamentalist militias, including Osama bin Laden's al-Qaeda organization, used the war-torn frontier of Afghanistan as a training ground for future terrorist operations. Osama bin Laden is a member of a wealthy Saudi family that made its fortune in the construction of office buildings and hotels in Saudi Arabia and the Persian Gulf. Bin Laden had fought with the Afghans against the Soviets and was wealthy enough to provide the mujahideen with arms and supplies. He had left Afghanistan in 1990 after the Soviet withdrawal and moved to Sudan amid a bitter argument with the Saudi royal family over their decision to allow the United States to maintain a military presence in Saudi Arabia following the 1991 Gulf War. The idea of non-Muslim, and therefore infidel, troops having a permanent presence in the holiest of Islamic countries was abhorrent to bin Laden. Once in Sudan, he devoted himself to building his al-Qaeda network. The Saudis revoked his citizenship in 1994, and the Sudanese government asked him to leave after he became the prime suspect in a June 1996 truck bombing that killed nineteen U.S. soldiers at a barracks in Dhahran, Saudi Arabia. Bin Laden returned to the cave complexes in Afghanistan he had helped build while fighting the Soviets in the 1980s. He was welcomed by the Taliban and made Afghanistan al-Qaeda's base of operations for conducting a jihad (holy war) of terror against the West.

By embracing militant fundamentalist Islam, and by harboring the like-minded bin Laden, the Taliban led Afghanistan on a path that culminated in a clash with U.S. forces. Bin Laden's jihad against the West and his use of Afghanistan as his base of operations turned the country into an international battle zone once again. On October 7, 2001, after Mullah Omar's refusal to turn bin Laden over for the crimes of September 11, U.S.-led forces launched an air assault on Afghanistan to topple the Taliban government. Within a few weeks, Taliban and al-Qaeda forces were on the run, and Northern Alliance forces in association with the U.S.-led coalition entered Kabul on November 13.

Afghanistan Faces Problematic Future After the War on Terror

Immediately following the U.S.-led military action, the United Nations took several steps to stabilize war-ravaged Afghanistan. On December 5, 2001, the UN hosted a meeting of anti-Taliban Afghan factions in Bonn, Germany, to establish the parameters of an interim authority in Afghanistan, which was installed in Kabul on December 22. In June 2002, a Loya Jirga, or grand council, was held by the interim authority and the tribal chieftains, and Hamid Karzai, an ethnic Pashtun, was elected head of the Transitional Authority. Despite these movements toward legitimate government and a restoration of order, the Transitional Authority faced several challenges. Among them were the attempted assassinations of several government figures, the task of rounding up remaining members of the Taliban and al-Qaeda, and peacekeeping in a country with little or no police force and a heavily armed populace. Given the legacy of devastation from years of war, driven by both civil and foreign factors, and the rise of militant Islam, Afghanistan faces an uncertain future. Whether or not the Transitional Authority currently ruling Afghanistan can maintain order in the country remains to be seen. Awareness of the factors that have shaped Afghanistan's past played a key role in U.S. military operations: For example, having witnessed the effects of British and Russian interference in Afghanistan, the United States decided to use only a small number of ground forces in Operation Enduring Freedom in an attempt to avoid being perceived as an invading imperial army and to prevent spontaneous uprisings of the Afghan people. Similar care may make the process of rebuilding Afghanistan smoother and assure a more successful outcome, but history clearly shows the difficulty of creating a lasting, stable state in Afghanistan.

First, the tribal factor must be considered. The Northern Alliance, a mostly Uzbek and Tajik organization, provided a great deal of assistance to the U.S.-led coalition forces in the war on terror in Afghanistan. Hamid Karzai's appointment as transitional president fulfills the historical precedent of Pashtuns serving as Afghan heads of state, but it may not satisfy Uzbek and Tajik demands for political reward and desires for power in the government to come. Afghanistan may again suffer from infighting among tribal factions.

A second factor to be considered is the fact that many members of the Northern Alliance practice a fundamentalist version of Islam similar to the one practiced by the Taliban. If a power vacuum forms in the wake of another tribal uprising, as was the case in the early 1990s, Afghanistan may find itself subject to radical fundamentalists and global terrorists once again. Afghanistan may be torn apart by war among heavily armed rival fundamentalist factions. Peacekeeping forces in Afghanistan may be seen by some Islamic leaders as an infidel force of foreign invaders. Their continued presence and assistance in Afghan affairs could create the impression that the Karzai government is a puppet of Western interests and therefore illegitimate. Such a model has clear precedents in Afghan history, including several British-controlled regimes and the Soviet-backed PDPA.

Finally, Afghanistan has never had a popular, democratically elected government. Most of the nation's leaders throughout history have taken power either by coup or assassination. The tribal warlords, now heavily armed thanks to decades of constant war and foreign aid, are strongly resistant to central government and have submitted to it only when it serves their own purposes. No assurances have been forthcoming that a permanent government, if one manages to take shape, will be honored. There is no precedent for a democratic alternative to tribal warlordism, foreign interference, or Islamic fundamentalist rule in Afghanistan. The Afghan people must find a way to unite for a cause other than repelling a foreign invader and create a central, modern government despite years of devastation and a strong tendency toward giving rise to and harboring Islamic fundamentalists. They are unlikely to do so without massive international support, which might be viewed as further foreign interference. Afghanistan has the opportunity to break its long destructive cycle, but its history could prove to be insurmountable, and it may remain a world hot spot for years to come.

CHAPTER 1

A Turbulent History

Afghanistan's Troubled History

By Martin Ewans

Despite the fact that it won its independence from Britain in 1919, Afghanistan, throughout its history, has been dependent on the assistance of other governments. Martin Ewans, a British diplomat formerly stationed in Kabul, the capital of Afghanistan, and a prolific writer on Afghan history, traces Afghanistan's tumultuous past with an emphasis on the role that foreign aid, or lack thereof, has played in Afghan politics. Specifically, he argues that the United States's lukewarm interest in the region at the beginning of the Cold War gradually pushed Afghanistan into dependence on the Soviet Union for developmental assistance. He also describes how that turn of events precipitated the country's fall into chaos in the 1980s and 1990s.

Although Afghanistan won its independence from British control in 1919, it was not until a quarter century later that the Afghan and U.S. administrations, just about as geographically remote from each other as was possible, considered there was sufficient content in their official relations to an exchanging of diplomatic missions. Following World War II, Afghans were anxious to develop a relationship with what they saw as a strong, influential nation with sound anti-colonial credentials, but they found themselves rebuffed.

Keen to obtain external assistance for their postwar development, they approached the United States in 1947 for help with an ambitious hydroelectric and irrigation project on the country's longest river, the Helmand. There was, however, little enthusiasm for the scheme in Washington, and it was left to a private U.S. company, Morrison-Knudson, to assist in its construction. Money soon ran out, and a request for a $120-million loan from the Import-Export Bank was whittled down to an inadequate $23 million. Essential surveys were neglected or cut short, and relationships deteriorated. Salination and

Martin Ewans, "America and Afghanistan: A Troubled History," *The World & I*, March 2002, pp. 20–25. Copyright © 2002 by News World Communications, Inc. Reproduced by permission.

waterlogging compromised the project, dooming it, to a large extent, to failure.

From 1948 on, Afghanistan approached the United States for help in equipping and training its antiquated armed forces but was similarly cold-shouldered. In 1955, a final request was turned down by [then secretary of state] John Foster Dulles. This seemed odd in the context of his Cold War policy of constructing treaty relationships around the periphery of the Soviet Union and communist China as a safeguard against the spread of communism.

Although Afghanistan was well placed geographically as a buffer along the Soviet Union's southern frontiers, it was politically at odds with Pakistan, a linchpin of the Central Treaty Organization [an alliance between Iran, Pakistan, Turkey, and the United Kingdom that lasted from 1959 to 1979]. Unwisely in view of its landlocked position, Afghanistan had been supporting a movement among the Pashtun tribes for an independent state in the northwest region of Pakistan, contiguous to Afghanistan. Additionally, the United States was reluctant to incur any obligation to assist Afghanistan should it be threatened militarily by the Soviet Union. The country was felt to be too remote and exposed for any such guarantee to be successful.

Pushed Toward the Soviet Union

The reasons for the United States not becoming involved were rational enough, but they effectively delivered the country into the hands of the Soviet Union. In 1955, Moscow hastened to supply Afghanistan with arms and military training, as well as a generous program of economic development.

After some delay, the Americans changed tack and decided that Afghanistan should not be left exclusively to the communist bloc, so they, too, went into the business of developmental assistance. Among other projects, the United States and the Soviet Union cooperated to build a strategic network of roads across the country (which later facilitated the Soviet invasion), while the United States also concentrated on assisting the University of Kabul and Afghanistan's national airline, Ariana.

It was fortunate for American interests, although not for Afghanistan itself, that during the 1960s and '70s, the Soviets proceeded to overreach themselves. An independent, nonaligned, but friendly Afghanistan, closely associated in their sphere of interest, would have suited them well, but they could not resist the temptation to engage in subversion.

Military personnel who went to the Soviet Union for training were routinely indoctrinated, while the Soviet Union also supported the People's Democratic Party of Afghanistan (PDPA), a party founded in 1965 that was, in all but name, the Afghan Communist Party. The first communist president of Afghanistan, Nur Mohammed Taraki, was financially assisted by Moscow, and his successor, Hafizullah Amin, was almost certainly recruited by the KGB [the Soviet intelligence agency] while doing postgraduate studies in the United States.

When, therefore, the PDPA mounted a coup in April 1978 and established a communist regime in Afghanistan, the Soviets found that they had created a monster they could not control. Although they had doubts of the wisdom of establishing a communist regime in a country as feudal as Afghanistan, they did nothing to prevent it.

U.S. assistance to the University of Kabul was also in some respects counterproductive, in that it became a hotbed of unrest, where many students, bitter at the lack of employment opportunities, were attracted to the Left. Of the 21 men who constituted the first PDPA cabinet, no fewer than 10 had been educated in the United States and a mere 3 in the Soviet Union.

Within its first few months, the Afghan communist regime had so antagonized the populace that uprisings and mutinies occurred across the country. Dominated by the dogma that a communist revolution, once it had occurred, was irreversible, the Soviet Union finally decided that the only option was to invade, which it duly did at the end of 1979.

Against all expectation, its forces encountered tough and sustained guerrilla opposition. This soon necessitated decisions in Washington about the nature and extent of any assistance to the mujahideen, the "holy warriors" who formed the nucleus of resistance.

During the first few years, despite the suffering inflicted by the conflict, U.S. policy was to keep the Soviet wound bleeding by supplying sufficient arms to sustain the mujahideen, but not enough to defeat the Soviet occupation. The arms supplied were not American but clandestinely purchased secondhand Soviet armaments from such countries as Egypt and Israel (the latter had captured them during various wars with Arab states) that were shipped to the mujahideen via Pakistan.

In April 1985 the policy changed when Ronald Reagan issued National Security Directive No. 166, ordering the United States to use all available means to compel the Soviets to withdraw. Following this instruction, the CIA adopted two strategies, both highly risky, aimed at making life difficult for the Soviet occupiers.

The first strategy was to supply the mujahideen with 900 Stinger surface-to-air missiles, along with training in their operation. (Many of these missiles have never been recovered.) The second was to supply arms and training to Muslim resistance fighters in Pakistan.

Both strategies worked well. The Stingers hampered Soviet airpower, while the so-called Arab Afghans (none of whom were Afghans and by no means all Arabs) proved themselves not only committed but increasingly battle hardened. Their numbers eventually ran to at least 35,000 and, by some accounts, appreciably more. Among them was a young Saudi plutocrat, Osama bin Laden, who fought little himself but supplied finances, facilities, and, ultimately, leadership to the Arab Afghans from a base in Peshawar [Pakistan].

With the Soviet withdrawal from Afghanistan in 1989, international interest in that country quickly evaporated. The conflict had claimed the lives of one million Afghans. Though it had helped catalyze the dissolution of the Soviet Union and the end of the Cold War, this was an eminent case of there being no gratitude in politics. The survivors received little concern, although a large refugee population needed care. Agriculture and industry had been destroyed, and the country-side was booby trapped with millions of land mines.

The mujahideen were excluded from the negotiations leading to the Soviet withdrawal, and so there was no agreement on an acceptable postwar political settlement. Over several years they proceeded to compete for dominance, variously supported by Pakistan, Iran, and other neighboring states. Receiving little encouragement from the United States or elsewhere, the United Nations attempted some totally ineffectual mediation, while the scant humanitarian aid that was forthcoming was grossly inadequate for the country's needs.

The Rise of the Taliban

The next chapter in the saga was written in 1994. By now disillusioned by its clients among the mujahideen, Pakistan switched its support to a new movement, the Taliban, whose rank and file, as well as leaders, were mostly the products of radical Pakistani religious schools. The majority of Arab Afghans still in the region were happy to join its ranks and fight what they saw as a continuing religious war.

Despite official denials, there is no doubt that the Taliban received military support from Pakistan and financial support from Saudi Arabia. There is also the question of American involvement. Although direct support has not been proved and is on the whole unlikely, the United States welcomed the Taliban's arrival on the scene, seeing it as opposed to Iran and believing that it would stabilize the country and the region. The United States also set store on the Taliban's undertakings to end Afghanistan's significant cultivation and trafficking of narcotics.

Above all, with the fragmentation of the Soviet Union, central Asian oil and gas fields were potentially important to the global market. A U.S. company, UNOCAL, actively sought to build a pipeline from Turkmenistan to the Arabian Sea through Afghanistan.

However, Washington's optimism about the Taliban was soon shattered. It proved unable to extend its control over the whole country and to ensure sufficient security for a pipeline. Rather than suppress the drug trade, the Taliban proceeded to encourage it, to its own considerable profit.

In 1996 bin Laden was allowed to return to Afghanistan, where he trained and organized his Arab Afghans into an international terrorist network, aimed mainly against the United States and Saudi Arabia. The Taliban's brutal social and judicial policies, notably its treatment of women, aroused strong protest in the United States and elsewhere, effectively precluding a close relationship. Afghanistan under the Taliban became a pariah nation, left to suffer under a singularly repressive regime and a landscape that deteriorated during a prolonged drought. The Taliban threatened the stability of Pakistan (where it had enjoyed much sympathy), whose nuclear weapons would become a major threat to peace if they were to fall into the hands of extremists.

From the outset, therefore, the U.S. record in Afghanistan has been one of purposelessness, ambivalence, and neglect. It failed to prevent Afghanistan from coming under Soviet control and shunned it following the Soviet withdrawal, with the result that Afghanistan became ripe for the Taliban takeover. But its main error was in promoting the "Arab-Afghan" presence during the Soviet occupation. The moment of truth came in 1993, when it was found that the World Trade Center bombers were Afghanistan-trained militants.

Bin Laden subsequently used his militants to mount murderous attacks on U.S. targets overseas and finally on the World Trade Center on September 11, 2001. Many of them have formed cells around the world, posing a threat to the stability of governments that are vital for U.S. global interests. Unraveling and neutralizing bin Laden's network will take years of effort and immense amounts of money.

Singularly lacking in U.S. policy toward Afghanistan have been consistent, long-term planning based on reliable intelligence, and an appreciation of its importance in the context of America's global interests. At this point, after years of neglect, a major international effort is an absolute necessity.

The main issue, however, is wider than that. The bin Laden brand of terrorism is the product of twisted minds and a subculture of religious fanaticism. Such fanaticism would not find a sea in which to swim but for a growing resentment, verging on despair, among the wretched of the earth. This is directed at a world order under which a minority, mainly in Europe and North America, live in unprecedented affluence, while the great majority, not only in the Muslim world but more widely, are compelled to live in abject poverty. It is unlikely to be a coincidence that Afghanistan, which is probably more wretched than any other country in the world, has also been the seat of a global terrorist threat.

The Soviet Invasion and the Rise of Islamic Terrorism

By Michael Binyon

When the Soviet Union invaded Afghanistan in December 1979, it did so on the pretext of attempting to bring stability to a communist country. A little more than a decade later, Afghanistan was a war-torn, desolate nation with a history of much interference and little aid from foreign powers. Michael Binyon, diplomatic editor for the Times of London, *discusses how Afghanistan's conflict with the Soviet Union set the stage for the establishment and growth of the al-Qaeda terrorist network and the spread of terrorism to other countries.*

In Arabic, Al-Qaeda means "the base". It is the name adopted by the fanatical followers of Osama bin Laden, who pray, plot and train for terrorist operations. The name is appropriate: Afghanistan, the country [that sheltered] bin Laden, harbour[ed] the nest of vipers from which, for the past 20 years, terrorist poison has been hatched and spread around the world.

The poison can be traced directly to the Soviet invasion of Afghanistan in 1979, when Moscow sent troops across the border to prop up the shaky communist regime and instal Babrak Karmal as their puppet. The West, surprised and bemused, decided a direct military response was impossible. But Western intelligence services then decided on a fateful step: they would harness the outrage of pious Muslims and direct their armed fury against the Soviets.

Promoting a jihad proved astonishingly successful. Afghans are a fiece, warrior people, wily and brave. They do not lack zeal or patriotism. What they did lack in 1978 was arms and training. And the Central Intelligence Agency was quick to help: bazookas, rockets, shoulder-held Stinger missiles, guns and ammunition worth up to £2.17 billion

Michael Binyon, "The Roots of Afghanistan Conflict Lie in Soviet War," *The Times of London*, September 14, 2001. Copyright © 2001 by NI Syndication, London. Reproduced by permission.

[almost $4 million], were soon on their way, carried by mules across the mountains from Pakistan.

The arms were manna to the Mujahidin, the holy warriors who had embraced the fight preached by conservative Muslim teachers—with Western encouragement. Warlords soon set themselves up to claim control of sections of the country and take on the Soviet forces in the region. Adopting classic guerrilla hit-and-run tactics, the Mujahidin made the most of the rugged landscape and their endurance to harry the Russians and confine them largely to the towns.

The key to the warlords' success was their ability to invoke Allah while subsuming their own chronic rivalries in the greater fight against the Russian invader. Religious zeal was the motivating factor that drove on the fighters, even when they were outnumbered, and gave them a courage that did not fear death. It was perfect training for classic terrorist tactics.

And it worked. Soviet losses grew. Morale collapsed as the Russian troops, unsure why they were in such a hostile country, cowered in the towns and tried to protect themselves against an unseen enemy. The ferocity of the Mujahidin became a weapon of considerable psychological terror. Stories of Russian soldiers being flayed alive, castrated or skewered to death served to further reduce them as a fighting force.

Eventually, Mikhail Gorbachev, the Soviet leader, saw that the game was up: the Soviet forces withdrew and the communist regime, by then confined to the city of Kabul, collapsed.

Foreign Muslims Drawn to Afghan Conflict

The Mujahidin had won a great victory—and had proved the power of guerrilla warfare, tight organisation, ruthlessness and Islamic fervour. The lessons were learnt not only by native Afghans: the jihad had drawn to Afghanistan thousands of pious Muslims from other countries, determined to join the fight to liberate Islamic land from the godless invader.

Egyptians, Pakistanis, Saudis, Iranians and volunteers of other nationalities lived and trained with the Afghan warlords. Among them was Osama bin Laden, the young millionaire Saudi who forsook a life of ease to take up the Islamic cause. And the West, for some years, poured in money and arms in the mistaken hope that these could be used to secure a democratic government in Kabul.

Bin Laden and many others who went to Afghanistan, were transformed, spiritually and mentally. The Islamic cause became their life: and even before the Russians left, they broadened the scope of their struggle. It had to encompass not just Afghanistan but all Muslim countries, which they saw as oppressed by corrupt rulers or foreign occupiers.

Fighters went home to join underground movements in Egypt, Turkey, Algeria and Pakistan. The *Afghantsi*, as the Russians called them, became a network of radical extremists ready to take up arms to promote an Islamic state. The chance came early in Algeria. With the annulment of the 1992 election by the corrupt ruling National Liberation Front, Islamic groups were the only underground opposition to the Army generals who seized power.

The Islamic Salvation Front took the war to the countryside; but the Afghan veterans brought their deadly experience to an even more radical and ruthless organisation, the Armed Islamic Group. An Afghan veteran was among the founding members.

In Eygpt, the veterans were invited to lend their muscle to the Islamic Jihad, the group that assassinated President Sadat in 1981, taking over the organisation of some of the terrorist attacks on tourists, foreigners and Egyptian government figures. Egypt struck back vigorously, setting up military courts, hanging many of those caught and banning all legal expression of Islamic radicalism.

By now bin Laden had set up a base in Sudan, where an Islamist government came to power, directed from the shadows by its political *éminence grise* [underground agent] Hassan al-Turabi [leader of the Sudanese People's National Congress party]. He gathered around him many of the Afghan veterans and plotted operations against Muslim leaders seen as pro-Western. Eventually even Sudan found his presence uncomfortable and he was forced to move back to Afghanistan.

The Afghan network was also involved elsewhere. Bosnia was the first opportunity to penetrate the Balkans. Some of the Mujahidin moved there to bolster the embattled Muslim forces, until even the Yugoslav Muslims found them too extreme. Western intelligence suspects that they have also been active in Albania and Kosovo, especially in helping to train and to arm the Kosovo Liberation Army.

The network can be traced to almost all terrorist incidents in Muslim countries: bombings in Istanbul, kidnappings in Yemen, attacks on tourists in Egypt, Hezbollah operations in southern Lebanon, plots by Jaish Muhammad [an Islamic Terrorist group based in Pakistan] to kill King Hussein and foreigners in Jordan, the explosions at the American barracks in Saudi Arabia and the blowing up of USS *Cole* in Yemen.

Bin Laden and his Afghan veterans have also extended their operations. They moved into Somalia and the Horn of Africa after the American intervention there, determined to push the Americans out. They began recruiting sleeper agents in Europe and even in the United States. And, . . . the long arm of the Afghan conflict has reached right into New York.

The Rise of the Taliban

By Peter Marsden

In the mid-1990s, a group of militant Islamic fundamentalists calling them-selves the Taliban (a plural form of talib, *the Arabic word for "seeker of knowledge") swept through Afghanistan, imposing their rule on a nation that had been long plagued by war. Though its origins remain mysterious, the Tal-iban was able to conquer most of Afghanistan and to consolidate its power slowly throughout the 1990s. Peter Marsden, information coordinator of the British Agencies Afghanistan Group, traces the Taliban's rise from its earli-est military campaign in the Afghan city of Kandahar to the moment it was recognized by Pakistan, Saudi Arabia, and the United Arab Emirates as the legitimate government of Afghanistan. He argues that the oppressive regime was initially successful because it seemed to be the only alternative to the bit-ter fighting that had ravaged Afghanistan for decades.*

It appears that the Taliban began as a small spontaneous group in [the city of] Kandahar [in southern Afghanistan], perhaps in early 1994. Its members, who were described as religious students, are said to have felt outrage at the behaviour of the Mujahidin [Afghan Islamic Free-dom Figures] leaders fighting for power in the city and to have decided to take action to end what they saw as corrupt practices, drawing on Islam as a justification for their intervention.

How they moved from small group to major force is not clear. How-ever, it is thought likely that they were seen by elements outside Af-ghanistan as being potentially useful in promoting their various inter-ests, and that these elements decided it was worthwhile to provide them with some backing. The nature and extent of the backing re-ceived from outside has been the subject of much speculation. Pak-istan, the USA and Saudi Arabia have all been implicated.

It is none the less clear that they benefited considerably from the

Peter Marsden, *The Taliban: War and Religion in Afghanistan*. New York: Zed Books, Ltd., 2002. Copyright © 2002 by Peter Marsden. Reproduced by permission.

willingness of young people, both from the rural areas and from refugee camps on the Pakistan border, to join their ranks as they advanced through southern Afghanistan. They were also able to draw on a significant quantity of weaponry, either abandoned by retreating forces or found in the process of disarming the population.

The ideological underpinning of the movement has been a further cause for debate. There appears to be little doubt that the Islamic *madrasahs* [religious schools] in the refugee camps, where Islam has been taught on the basis of recitation of the Koran, have proved to be fertile ground for recruits. It is also likely that the orphanages operated in the refugee camps, with funding from Saudi Arabia, the Gulf States and the Mujahidin parties, will have produced strong adherents to radical Islam, some of whom will have been attracted by the call to arms issued by the Taliban. Also evident is the role of the Islamist parties in Pakistan in training young people in their various educational establishments, and the contribution these establishments have made to the expansion of the Taliban movement. Equally unclear is the question of how the Taliban forces have received their military training. . . .

The Emergence of the Taliban

The Taliban appeared to emerge out of nowhere when they first came to the world's notice in October 1994. Their arrival on the Afghan military scene coincided with an initiative by the government of Pakistan to dispatch a trade convoy through Afghanistan, via Kandahar and Herat, to Turkmenistan. As the convoy entered Afghanistan, travelling north from Quetta, it was attacked by an armed group. Immediately, another group came to the rescue and fought off the attackers. These were the Taliban.

After allowing the convoy to proceed, the Taliban moved on Kandahar and took the city with almost no resistance. Kandahar had witnessed virtual anarchy for the previous two years, as a number of Mujahidin groups fought for control. The Taliban were able to seize the faction leaders, killing some and imprisoning others. Having taken the city, they called on the population to surrender their weapons at a designated place and to cooperate with the new authorities in bringing peace to the area. The people duly complied.

The Taliban simultaneously announced that it was their mission to free Afghanistan of its existing corrupt leadership and to create a society that accorded with Islam. They issued decrees in which they required men to wear turbans, beards, short hair and *shalwar kameez* [a long top and trousers worn with a scarf] and women to wear the *burqa*, a garment that covers the entire body, including the face. Men were strongly encouraged to pray five times a day, ideally in the mosque.

Women were advised that it was their responsibility to bring up the next generation of Muslims. To this end, they were prohibited from working. It was also made clear that the education of girls would have to await the drawing up of an appropriate Islamic curriculum by religious scholars, and that this process could start only when the Taliban had control of the whole country. Other decrees banned music, games and any representation of the human or animal form. In order to enforce these bans, televisions and tapes were symbolically displayed in public places.

Early Military Success

The remarkable success of the Taliban in bringing order to Kandahar earned them considerable popularity and this, building on popular superstition and combined with their distinctive white turbans and obvious religious fervour and purity, lent them an almost supernatural aura. When they moved westwards from Kandahar, their reputation had already travelled before them and they were able to clear the main road of armed groups and bandits with great ease. As they captured positions they seized abandoned weaponry, some of it left in great haste, and encouraged people to join the ranks of their fighters.

Over the winter of 1994–95, the Taliban were able to repeat this pattern many times over and, by February 1995, they were positioned on hilltops overlooking the southern suburbs of Kabul, having taken almost half of Afghanistan. They had even managed to secure the speedy evacuation of Charasyab, to the south of the capital, from which warlord Gulbuddin Hekmatyar had launched rockets on the city for three years. As they approached Kabul from the south-west they captured the western suburbs at the invitation of the Shi'a [a minority sect of Islam in Afghanistan] group, Hisb-e-Wahdat, which feared a worse outcome if Afghanistan's defense minister Masoud's forces were to attack. In the course of the military operation the Shi'a leader, Abdul Ali Mazari, was taken by the Taliban and he died a few days later in their custody, for reasons that remain unclear.

The occupation of western Kabul proved to be short-lived, however. Government troops launched a major offensive and were able to retake the area within a month of its capture by the Taliban. They were also able to push the Taliban out of Charasyab to positions out of rocket range of Kabul. Thereafter, there was a virtual stalemate between the forces of the Taliban and those of the government, at least in relation to Kabul, until September 1996. During the intervening 18 months, the capital experienced a period of relative calm until the Taliban were able to recover Charasyab and also capture new positions in October 1995. These enabled them to shell and rocket the city while

Hekmatyar's troops simultaneously blocked commercial and aid convoys from the east. The northern route to Mazar-i-Sharif also remained closed, due to the long-standing conflict between the government and Dostam [leader of the Uzbek minority in northern Afghanistan].

The winter of 1995–96 was a particularly harsh one for Kabul as food and fuel shortages and spiralling inflation took their toll on a highly impoverished people. Humanitarian agencies pulled out the stops to get relief supplies to the capital, but the task was far from easy. Memories of this hardship were a factor in the relative ease with which the Taliban subsequently took Kabul in September 1996.

While the Taliban were endeavouring to take Kabul, there was also intense military activity in western Afghanistan. The city of Herat was under the control of Ismail Khan [former leader of a resistance movement against the Soviets], who was allied to the government. He had taken Herat Province in April 1992, when the Soviet-backed government had fallen, and had gradually increased his dominion of influence over the western provinces of Farah and Nimroz, to the south, and Badghis, to the north-west. When the Taliban moved west from Kandahar, they sought to take the entire road through Herat to the Turkmenistan border. However, their way was blocked at Shindand, about 120 km south of Herat, where there was a large military airbase. Ismail Khan's forces mined the approaches to the airbase in an effort to withstand the forward advance of the Taliban. They were successful in holding off the attack, but had to contend with a wave of men willing to martyr themselves for the cause as they rushed forward over the minefields. This aspect of Taliban strategy added further to the image of invincibility that went before them.

Over the ensuing months, there was a stand-off between the forces of the Taliban and Ismail Khan at Delaram, on the border between the provinces of Farah and Helmand. Then, in August 1995, Ismail Khan's forces took the initiative and advanced towards Kandahar. They moved with remarkable speed at first and posed a serious threat to the city. However, they were halted by the Taliban at Girishk, about 120 km west of Kandahar, and then pushed back. The Taliban kept going and, within a relatively short space of time, had taken Shindand and walked into Herat without a fight, entering it on 5 September 1995. Based on prior agreement between the Taliban and Dostam, the latter's forces lent air support to the advance.

There has been much speculation as to why Ismail Khan gave in so easily to the Taliban and effectively handed over Herat to them. Rumours at the time that there had been differences between Ismail Khan and the central government in Kabul, which had led to Ismail Khan's resignation or dismissal from the post of governor, cannot be substantiated. Another rumour in circulation was that Ismail Khan wished to avoid the destruction of a city he had taken three years to rebuild and that he may not have felt able to count on the support of the population who, having enjoyed a period of peace, were reluctant to take up arms again. The fact that the Taliban had, up to that point, a reputation for behaving relatively well when taking new areas—they did not engage in looting, rape or mindless destruction—may have strengthened an assessment that resistance by the population on any scale could not be relied upon.

Taliban Rule in Herat

When the Taliban took Herat they issued edicts on the dress and behaviour of the population, as they had done in Kandahar, ordered the closure of all the girls' schools, and placed a ban on women working. The statue of a horse in the city centre was decapitated because, by representing the animal form, it was seen as being inconsistent with Islam. The Taliban conducted house-to-house searches to disarm the population.

The edicts relating to female access to education and employment had a greater impact than they had had in Kandahar. In Kandahar, the administrative infrastructure had effectively collapsed by the time the Taliban arrived and there were few girls' schools in operation. There were also very few opportunities for women to seek employment outside the home. However, in Herat city in 1994 there was a reported school population of 21,663 girls and 23,347 boys. By contrast, in the rural areas, 1,940 girls were attending school as compared with 74,620 boys (Save the Children Fund UK, 1994). A significant proportion of the teachers were women and it proved necessary to close many boys' schools as a result. Further, much of the population of Herat had lived as refugees in Iran, where female access to education had been provided as a right. The bans on girls being educated, pending the introduction of a new and more appropriate curriculum, and on women working, therefore had a significant impact.

The capture of Herat by the Taliban was felt to be a military occupation, not only because of the restrictions placed on female access to education and employment but also because, culturally and linguistically, the predominantly Pushtun and rural Taliban were very different from the Persian-speaking Heratis, with their long aesthetic and liberal traditions.

During the early months of Taliban rule in Herat, long queues were reported outside the Iranian consulate as large numbers applied for visas for Iran. Many of these were educated professionals, a proportion of whom had been working in the various government ministries.

There was an obvious slowing down in the construction sector, reducing the opportunities for people to engage in daily labouring work and accelerating the process of return to Iran. The repatriation programme from Iran to western Afghanistan ground to a standstill.

Humanitarian agencies sought to engage in dialogue with the Taliban in Herat as they had done in Kandahar. In the latter city, it had proved possible to secure authority for women to work in the health sector and this authority had been extended when the Taliban took Herat. However, the agencies in Herat were not able to achieve any modification of the ban on women working in non-health-related posts or a reversal of the closure of girls' schools.

The Taliban Take the Capital City

Following the capture of Herat the Taliban made few gains until, a year later, they suddenly marched into Jalalabad, on 11 September 1996. Again, there was minimal resistance as the Mujahidin leaders who had composed the Nangarhar *shura* [Islamic religious or political council] opted to leave without much of a fight. The Taliban then surprised all observers by forcing themselves through the apparently impenetrable Sarobi Gorge. After a few days of intense fighting in the eastern suburbs of Kabul, they walked into the capital on 26 September with scarcely a shot being fired. Shockwaves were then felt throughout the world when ex-President [Muhammad] Najibullah and his brother, who was visiting him, were seized from the protection of the UN compound, within a few hours of the Taliban entering the city, and hanged in a public place. It is still not known whether this hanging was authorised by the Taliban leadership or carried out spontaneously by enthusiastic followers, or whether others, with old scores to settle, took the opportunity created by the situation to wreak their revenge. It was rumoured that the atrocity arose from old antagonisms within the PDPA [the People's Democratic Party of Afghanistan—a Communist party]. Others wondered whether Najibullah's years as head of the secret police had played a part.

The population of Kabul would, by this stage, have been apprehensive of a further prolonged siege of the capital. Many had already sold even their most basic possessions and were nearing destitution. When the Taliban entered there was therefore considerable relief and a hope that there might, at last, be peace and the possibility of an improvement in the local economy. It is likely that [Burhanuddin] Rabbani [president of Afghanistan 1992–1996] and Masoud were aware of this view amongst the population, and this may have been a factor in their decision not to fight for every last inch of Kabul. The aura of invincibility held by the Taliban may have created an additional concern that the government forces would be unwilling to put up a fight. The government may also have calculated that opposition to the Taliban would grow once they had taken the capital, and Masoud made this view explicit in a number of subsequent statements.

However, the Taliban did not wait to consolidate their hold on Kabul but moved immediately north. Within a few days they were facing Dostam's troops at the top of the Salang Pass, which divides north from south Afghanistan, and Masoud's forces at the entrance to the Panjshir Valley, which had witnessed much of the resistance to the Soviet occupation. The Taliban sought to negotiate a peace deal with Dostam. Dostam and Masoud responded by opting to shelve their longstanding enmity and to form a military alliance; their combined forces were then able to push the Taliban back to positions just north of Kabul, where a new stalemate developed.

The Taliban responded to the alliance by opening up a new front in north-western Afghanistan. In October 1996 they took Badghis Province, which Dostam had seized in September 1995 following the Taliban capture of Herat. Heavy fighting ensued between the forces of Dostam and the Taliban in eastern Badghis. The population of Herat were said to be apprehensive of a Dostam victory because of the reputation of Dostam's forces for looting and raping in the wake of battle.

In Kabul, the Taliban proceeded to issue the same edicts as they had done in Kandahar and Herat. However, it soon became clear that there was to be a greater degree of enforcement of the Taliban requirements, particularly that men should pray at their local mosques rather than individually and that the dress codes for men and women, including long beards, *shalwar kameez* and turbans for men and the *burqa* for women, should be strictly observed.

There was also a downturn in the economy as there had been in Herat. This was in spite of easier access for trade than there had been during the previous siege of Kabul (mitigated by [Afghan warlord Gulbuddin] Hekmatyar entering the government a few weeks before the Taliban takeover), and in contrast to the mushrooming of the Kandahar economy during the post-Taliban period. In the case of Kabul, this may have been a consequence of many government servants suddenly losing their jobs or being paid only very irregularly when the Taliban took control. The departure, with the ousted government, of what little was left of the more affluent element of Kabul society may have accelerated this process. Certainly the Kabul money market, which provides a good indicator of the health of the economy, responded very positively to the Taliban takeover during the first week or so, but the afghani [the main monetary unit in Afghanistan] then fell in value again. Subsequent problems, with Dostam printing his own banknotes and the ousted government flooding the market with newly printed notes, caused spiralling inflation and a virtual collapse of the afghani.

The Population Flees Taliban Rule

Whether for economic reasons or fear of renewed conflict, there was a significant outward flow of people from Jalalabad and Kabul following the arrival of the Taliban. Ten thousand people left for Pakistan from Jalalabad in September 1996, some in direct response to a bombing raid launched by government forces. A further 50,000 fled to Pakistan from Kabul between October and December 1996 in response to Taliban restrictions and a growing climate of fear. Provision was made for the new arrivals at Nasir Bagh camp near Peshawar. As in Herat, this departure further weakened the government and reduced the pool of skilled professionals able to run an administration.

During the early months after the takeover of Kabul, the Taliban gave every indication of having overextended themselves. It proved difficult for outside organisations and diplomatic missions to be clear as to the nature of the internal decision-making process. There were inconsistencies in some of the public statements made, which created concern and confusion. Some of the soldiers in the streets appeared to be acting in the absence of any clear chain of command.

It was also evident that the Taliban regarded the population of Kabul as being very different from those living in other conquered areas. Many of them had their roots in rural traditions and gave the impression of seeing Kabul as corrupt and decadent. The behaviour of the foot-soldiers at times reflected this attitude, and led to a number of incidents on which [human rights watch group] Amnesty International reported. The Taliban leadership gave every indication that they regretted these early excesses and Mullah Omar, the Taliban leader in Kandahar, issued an appeal on Radio Voice of Shari'a for his followers to treat the population of Kabul kindly.

There were also tensions in Kabul arising from Ahmed Shah Masoud's statements that he hoped the population would rise up against the Taliban. The Taliban were reported to have conducted house-to-house searches for those rumoured to be sympathetic to Masoud, and a number of people were arrested. Because of the absence of records as to who was held where, there was concern over apparent disappearances.

Three months after their capture of Kabul, the Taliban made another attempt to move north. This time they were successful in taking the settlements between Kabul and the Salang Pass, but they avoided some of the problems they had faced from insurrections during their earlier attempt by evacuating the area. Over a hundred thousand people were sent to Kabul as refugees while the Taliban consolidated their hold.

The Taliban's Decisive Blow

As 1997 took its course the numbers entering Kabul from the north rose gradually to 200,000. These had to fend largely for themselves, staying with relatives or finding some way of surviving. Appeals were made by the United Nations High Commissioner for Refugees for people to be allowed to return to their homes north of the capital, but these were rejected. The Taliban were totally focused on their objective of taking the whole country and did not want to take any risks.

The early months of 1997 were characterised by a stalemate as fighting continued on a number of fronts. To the south of the Salang Pass, Hisb-e-Wahdat withstood the efforts of the Taliban to cross the Shibar Pass and so move west and then north over an alternative route to the blocked Salang Pass. Masoud's forces also kept the Taliban busy in and around the Panjshir Valley, to the east. Casualties on both sides were said to be high. In the north-west of Afghanistan, at Ghormach in Badghis, the fighting was said to be even more intense as the Taliban attempted to move into Dostam's territory. The Taliban even encountered problems in the area they had already conquered as Haji Qadir, the ousted leader of the former Nangarhar *shura*, organised an incursionary movement from Pakistan into Kunar and Nangarhar until he was expelled by Pakistan on 14 May.

This stalemate was suddenly and dramatically broken when one of Dostam's generals, Abdul Malik, who controlled the province of Faryab to the immediate east of the Badghis front-line, announced on 19 May that he had defected to the Taliban. He then moved on Mazar and took it, without a fight, on 24 May, Dostam having fled to Uzbekistan. The following day he allowed the Taliban to enter the city.

The Taliban leadership responded quickly to the victory by sending many of their top people to Mazar. The first country to announce that it had decided to recognise the Taliban as the legitimate government of Afghanistan was Pakistan, which promptly dispatched an ambassador. Saudi Arabia and the United Arab Emirates quickly followed Pakistan's example and accorded the Taliban recognition.

The U.S.-Led Attack on Afghanistan and the Fall of the Taliban

By Stephen Tanner

Following the September 11, 2001, attacks on the World Trade Center and the Pentagon, U.S. and British authorities discovered several links between the hijackers and the al-Qaeda terrorist network run by Osama bin Laden. Afghanistan quickly became a prime military target when the Taliban, a group of Islamic fundamentalists who controlled most of the country, refused to hand over bin Laden to U.S. officials. Within a matter of a few weeks, a U.S.-led coalition of several nations mounted an attack on Afghanistan that managed to overthrow the Taliban and put al-Qaeda in disarray. Stephen Tanner, a military historian and freelance writer, traces the 2001 U.S.-led war in Afghanistan. In the following selection, the author argues that the relatively quick victory achieved by the U.S.-led force was partially due to the Taliban's underestimation of the vast military capability of the United States and to the popular uprising against the oppressive Taliban regime by the Afghan people.

[A fter the September 11, 2001, attacks on the World Trade Center and the Pentagon] it only took a day for U.S. intelligence to identify many of the September 11 terrorists, provide headshots, their recent movements, and to confirm their connection to Osama Bin Laden's Al Qaeda organization. The flurry of communications intercepts and data tracked by the CIA, FBI, and NSA prior to the attack had revealed that something was about to happen; they just hadn't known what, where, or how big. It was only after the attacks that all

Stephen Tanner, *Afghanistan: A Military History from Alexander the Great to the Fall of the Taliban*. New York: Da Capo Press, 2002. Copyright © 2002 by Stephen Tanner. Reproduced by permission of the publisher.

the pieces came together over the remains of nineteen suicidal Arab hijackers, fifteen of them from Saudi Arabia, who from different locations on the East Coast had coordinated the four separate operations.

Congress appropriated $40 billion for antiterror operations, though in fact, Bush received an open checkbook on the fourteenth when the Senate voted unanimously to authorize "all necessary and appropriate force." The president then laid down the gauntlet to the world at large: "You're either with us or against us." He sought to create a greater coalition of nations in support of the U.S. response to September 11 than his father had assembled for the Gulf War in 1990.

Going After Bin Laden

The first step was to demand that the Taliban government in Afghanistan hand over Osama Bin Laden. [Taliban leader] Mullah Omar instinctively refused. A delegation from Pakistan, headed by ISI [Pakistan's Intelligence Organization] general Faiz Gilani, traveled to Kandahar to convince Omar to give up Bin Laden and his Al Qaeda associates. The Taliban attempted to bargain, demanding diplomatic recognition, cessation of foreign support for the Northern Alliance, and a resumption of foreign aid. Omar also demanded "convincing evidence" of Bin Laden's involvement. At this time an odd dynamic occurred in the Islamic world, wherein a majority of people claimed to believe in Bin Laden's innocence, even while his photo was paraded at demonstrations and displayed as large posters in families' living rooms. He had become an outlaw superstar to much of the Islamic world, a status reinforced rather than dimmed by America's resolve to get him, in Bush's words, "dead or alive.". . .

World reaction to the September 11 attacks was a combination of deep sympathy for the loss of so many innocents, fear of some kind of berserk American response, and pragmatic interest now that the U.S. was fully engaged against Islamic radicals. Israeli Prime Minister Ariel Sharon canceled peace talks he had scheduled with Yasser Arafat of the Palestinian Authority on the theory that after September 11 U.S. pressure to compromise with the Arabs would disappear. Russia offered its support to the United States while anticipating its own battles against Islamic extremists in Chechnya would no longer be criticized. India stiffened its back against the Muslim terrorists who had been waging war in Kashmir. [The Central Asian Republic of] Uzbekistan, Tajikistan, and Kyrgyzstan welcomed U.S. emissaries requesting base facilities, pleased to receive aid in return and a new power in the region to balance the looming presence of Russia.

The country in the most ticklish position was Pakistan, which had all but created the Taliban and had continued to support it until September

11. (Pakistani shipments through Jalalabad continued into October, though were said to be the final remnants of previous commitments.) General Pervez Musharraf, who had taken power in a coup in 1999 now abandoned the Taliban and offered the U.S. his full support. Pakistan had been shunned by the U.S. since test-firing a nuclear bomb in 1994 and now saw an opportunity to regain an ally, especially, if need be, for its continuing struggle against India. Musharraf had also been appalled at the September 11 attacks and had found that the Taliban, like a Frankenstein monster, had been slipping out of his control.

On September 20, 2001 President Bush addressed the U.S. Congress and public with an eloquent, determined call to arms. Many observers noted that the president, formerly known for jocularity and tonguetied non sequiturs, now seemed transformed, with a steely gaze and unmistakable resolve. "The Taliban," he said, "must act and act immediately." His widely lauded speech concluded:

> The course of this conflict is not known yet its outcome is certain. Freedom and fear, justice and cruelty, have always been at war. And we know that God is not neutral between them. . . . We'll meet violence with patient justice, assured of the rightness of our cause and confident of the victories to come. In all that lies before us, may God grant us wisdom and may he watch over the United States of America.

Operation Enduring Freedom

The Taliban mullahs responded with a call for holy war "if infidels invade an Islamic country." During the next two weeks, American forces moved into place while fuel and munitions were stockpiled at airbases from Spain to the Indian Ocean. Acting upon reports of famine, and anxious not to antagonize the broader world of Islam, the United States organized a massive food lift into Afghanistan, dropping crates of packaged meals. The code name for the forthcoming military campaign, "Infinite Justice," was canceled after critics pointed out its religious overtone, as if Jehovah was about to come after Allah. Administration officials had already been advised not to use the word "crusade." The code name for the U.S. military effort was changed on September 25 to "Enduring Freedom."

Early in October, the U.S. revealed to a council of NATO nations the results of its investigations into the September 11 attacks. Proof of Al Qaeda responsibility was irrefutable. British Prime Minister Tony Blair was foremost among champions of the American cause. "This is a battle with only one outcome," he declared. "Our victory, not theirs." On October 6, Bush announced that "Full warning has been given, and time is running out."

The next day, October 7, American and British forces attacked Afghanistan. Fifteen land-based bombers and twenty-five carrier-based fighter bombers soared over the Hindu Kush [Mountains of Afghanistan] while fifty Tomahawk missiles were launched from U.S. ships and British submarines in the Arabian Sea. Targeted were Taliban compounds, command centers, and airfields. In the first hours, the small Taliban air force was destroyed on the ground, as was its supply of SA-2 and SA-3 antiaircraft missiles.

As the smoke cleared, an anonymous messenger dropped a package at the door of the Kabul bureau of Al Jazeera, an Arab television network based in Qatar. Inside was a videotaped speech from Osama Bin Laden. Dressed in camouflage and standing before a rock face with a rifle at his side, he began: "Here is America struck by God Almighty in one of its vital organs, so that its greatest buildings are destroyed." He went on to speak of eighty years of Islamic humiliation, starving Iraqi children, Israeli tanks in Palestine, and U.S. atomic attacks on Japan. He concluded his speech by renewing his call for global jihad:

> The wind of change is blowing to remove evil from the peninsula of Muhammed, peace be upon him. As to America, I say to it and its people a few words: I swear to God that America will not live in peace before peace reigns in Palestine, and before all the army of infidels depart the land of Muhammed, peace be upon him. God is the greatest and glory be to Islam.

U.S. airstrikes continued with B-1s flying from Diego Garcia, and huge, exotic B-2 stealth bombers crossing half the world at high subsonic speed from Whiteman Air Force Base, Missouri. Navy F-14s and F-18s flying from the *Enterprise* and *Carl Vinson* helped to obliterate seven Taliban compounds, though they appeared to have been hastily evacuated. AC-130 Spectre gunships arrived in the theater. These low-flying propellor aircraft bristled with 25mm Gatling guns and 40mm and 105mm cannon, all computer coordinated to focus on a ground target while the plane circled above it.

The airstrikes quickly became controversial as a United Nations compound in Kabul was accidentally hit, killing four workers; and, according to Taliban reports, dozens of civilians were killed in a village called Karam. On that same day, another errant 2,000-pound bomb hit a residence in the capital, decimating a family. Abdul Haq, a famous former mujahideen leader who had operated against the Soviets around Kabul, said that the bombing was counterproductive in that it would only rally Afghans around the Taliban. Part of the problem was that the United States soon became short of visible military targets. Pakistan's President Musharraf had insisted that the Americans not bomb Taliban troop positions facing the Northern Alliance near Kabul for fear that another Tajik-Uzbek takeover of the capital would only duplicate the 1992 situation that had resulted in a civil war with the Pashtuns. . . .

Attacking the Front Line

On October 21, U.S. warplanes began to pound Taliban frontline positions north of Kabul. Until then, Taliban soldiers had actually gone to the front for safety since the Americans were bombing everywhere else but there. Northern Alliance troops who had fought for years without air support now thrilled to the sight of history's strongest air force coming to their aid. The Americans employed 5,000-pound laser-guided "bunker busters" as well as 2,000-pound "smart bombs" (Joint Direct Attack Munitions, or JDAMs) guided by lasers or satellites. [US Secretary of Defense Ronald] Rumsfeld announced—more for Pakistani than American ears—why the U.S. had switched its effort to the front lines instead of persisting in attacks on the practically nonexistent Taliban infrastructure in the south. "It happens," he said, "that they are arrayed against, for the most part, Northern Alliance forces north of Kabul and in the northwest portion of the country." The Northern Alliance pitched in with rocket, artillery, and tank fire, answered in kind by the Taliban. Heavy machine-gun fire was exchanged by both sides across the rugged ridge lines and valleys. . . .

After a month of the U.S. bombing campaign, rumblings began to reach Washington from Europe, the Mideast, and Pakistan, from where Musharraf had requested that the bombing cease. Having begun the war with the greatest imaginable reservoir of moral authority, the U.S. was on the verge of letting it slip away through high-level attacks using the most ghastly inventions its scientists could come up with. Meanwhile, Taliban troops manned clear front lines, occasionally jeering at their Northern Alliance counterparts, while fifty thousand American forces in the theater (half naval) plus some two million in reserve in the U.S. and around the world seemed reluctant to engage.

Renewed Support

On November 10 President Bush went to New York, where the wreckage of the World Trade Center still smoldered with underground fires, to address the United Nations. "Every nation has a stake in this cause," he reminded the assembled delegates. "As we meet, the terrorists are planning more murder, perhaps in my country, perhaps in yours." His words had impact. Most of the world renewed its support for the American effort, including commitments of material help from Germany, France, Italy, Japan, and other countries. To that point the United States and Britain, along with Canada and Australia, had been most active in the battle. One problem that prevented the international community from showing a more solid military front was that American air- and sea-lift capacity, its air and naval power, and existing base network were far superior to those of its allies. When European troops eventually arrived in Kabul, they disembarked from Ukrainian commercial airliners. In the Pentagon the realization set in that U.S. forces could act faster and more decisively without having to coordinate with a broad coalition of inferior military establishments.

But as winter approached, U.S. military planners anticipated that operations, including air strikes, would become more difficult. There was also a debate whether to pause during the Muslim holy month of Ramadan, due to begin in mid-November. The food airlift had petered out amid Taliban accusations that the packaged meals were poisoned and U.S. counterwarnings that the Taliban might poison them just to prove their point. The propaganda rationale for the food drops had in any case disappeared since Pakistani Pashtuns had not risen en masse in support of their Taliban cousins across the border. The Bush administration repeatedly warned the U.S. public to prepare for a long, hard war. Its estimate, however, was mistaken.

Taking the Cities

By early November 2001, the Tajik mujahideen leader, Ismail Khan, had returned to his old stomping grounds in the west around Herat, and the Uzbek warlord Abdul Rashid Dostum had reorganized his loyal former troops in the north. Haji Mohaqiq mobilized fighters from the Hazarajat [the domain of the Hazaras desendants of the Mongols] within the Hindu Kush, where the Taliban, like the Soviets before them, had been largely reluctant to go. While Bush had been making his plaintive appeal before the United Nations, General Osta Atta Muhammad of the Northern Alliance had moved on the northern Afghan city of Mazar-i-Sharif from the east, cooperating with Dostum, who had placed his forces to the south. They overran the airport and then took Mazar after fighting for half an hour. The Taliban defenders defected or surrendered. Those who fled west were met by Ismail Khan, leading his forces to the scene northward from Herat. Many Taliban eagerly accepted Uzbek or Tajik protection against the Mongol-featured Hazaras, who remembered the Taliban slaughter of six thousand of their kinsmen in 1997.

In the northeast, Northern Alliance forces moved against the Taliban-held cities of Taliqan and Kunduz. Taliqan came under siege while Tajik commanders advised the Taliban leaders inside to surrender. One Taliban general, Abdullah Gard, went over to his Tajik opponent, Daoud Khan, with at least one thousand men. On November 11 the city fell without bloodshed, the remaining Pashtun defenders simply defecting to their longtime enemies. Northern Alliance troops rushing toward Taliban trenchlines north of Taliqan, however, were knocked back by a torrent of fire. Many Taliban in the north were foreign volunteers, more fanatic than the Pashtun and not so welcomed by Afghans if they surrendered. U.S. aircraft carefully roamed the skies, seeking targets of opportunity or responding to calls from Special Forces or USAF spotters on the ground.

British Special Air Service (SAS) commandos were also in Afghanistan. In one action reported by the London *Times* and the *Telegraph*, a "Sabre" team of about sixty men stormed a tunnel holding an equivalent number of Taliban fighters inside. The tally was two wounded SAS at the entrance and two more wounded in the subterranean gunfight, against eighteen dead Taliban and over forty captured. . . .

Taking Kabul

The Northern Alliance made rapid progress across the Shomali plain leading to Kabul. Taliban lines had been abandoned, some men retreating, others defecting and many making off for their homes. The city of Herat succumbed to Ismail Khan's men that afternoon, after six thousand Taliban had defected to the ex-mujahideen commander. Simultaneously, Kabul was officially abandoned by the Taliban, the remaining troops urged on by a message from Mullah Omar: "Take to the mountains. Defending the cities with front lines that can be targeted from the air will cause us terrible loss." Taliban columns retreating south of the city were hit by U.S. fighter bombers.

The Northern Alliance had promised the United States (representing Pakistan's worries) to halt two miles north of Kabul rather than enter the city and attempt to set up a new government. "We will encourage our friends to head south," said Bush, "but not into the city of Kabul itself." But after five years of battling the Taliban, the temptation to enter the capital was too great to ignore. On November 13, Northern Alliance troops marched into Kabul to the jubilation of many of its citizens. Though fears of urban fighting or large-scale atrocities were not realized, there were some ugly incidents. Several Taliban stragglers were humiliated, beaten, or executed. In one incident, six Arab and Pakistani Taliban sprung an ambush, two firing from up in the branches of a tree. After Northern Alliance troops killed them, their bodies were gleefully mutilated by citizens of Kabul, venting years of frustration.

The general scene was less gruesome. The harsh theocracy of Taliban rule had never sat well in Kabul, a city which had received a taste of modernization during the Soviet occupation and had always stood apart from the strict fundamentalism of the Afghan countryside. By way of greeting the Northern Alliance's arrival, music blared in the streets for the first time in years, and flowers were strewn in the path of tanks. Some women even took off their veils, though this was considered risky in case the Taliban suddenly returned, and because their liberators, as some women quickly remembered, were not Western troops but those who had formerly called themselves "soldiers of God."

Jalalabad was abandoned by the Taliban at the same time as Kabul, and Yunis Khalis, leader of one of the former Peshawar-based parties of mujahideen, quickly claimed control. Ismail Khan reorganized Herat while Dostum flew his flag again over Mazar-i-Sharif. Rumors abounded that Gulbuddin Hekmatyar would return from exile in Iran to reclaim his eastern Ghilzai territory south of Kabul. Aside from the lamented Massoud, all the major players of the Soviet war and the mujahideen civil war were reassuming their positions. Presidents Bush and Musharraf had meanwhile urgently complained to Rabbani, political head of the Northern Alliance, about his troops breaking their promise not to enter Kabul. Rabbani stated that his men were only there for security reasons and that only three thousand would remain in the capital.

The northern half of Afghanistan had been cleared of Taliban except for the city of Kunduz, thirty-five miles west of Taliqan. There, remaining units of Pashtun Taliban congregated with diehard foreign volunteers and elements of Osama Bin Laden's Al Qaeda. The Northern Alliance surrounded the city and sent in congenial offers to surrender. On November 13, Tajik troops approached to accept the defection of an Afghan Pashtun contingent, but were suddenly fired upon by foreign volunteers who had learned of the plan. The Northern Alliance men scrambled back to their trenches after suffering several casualties. Present in Kunduz were scores of Arabs as well as Punjabis, Chinese, Chechens, and Indonesians, plus hundreds of Pakistanis and a scattering of other nationals who had signed on to the Taliban's cause.

Amid warnings from journalists such as Rohde of the *New York Times* who wrote, "the country's political map is beginning to look ominously like the map of 1989," America and Britain rushed in elite troops, eight C-130s delivering 160 Green Berets and Royal Marines to Bagram air base north of Kabul on November 15. The problem was that the Taliban, for all its flaws, had actually established order in a country that had completely lacked it in the post-Soviet years when warlords vied for power. If the Taliban collapsed it was now incumbent on the Americans and their British allies not to allow the same situation to resume.

Suspicion that the Taliban had disappeared before they could truly be defeated was reinforced on November 19, when four Western journalists were shot in cold blood on the mountainous road to Kabul from Jalalabad. According to a surviving witness, a gunman had said, "What did you think? It's the end of the Taliban? The Taliban are still here." The Tajik political leader Rabbani, meanwhile, assured the U.S. that he would not try to form a government, pending the decision of a council of Afghan leaders America had assembled in Bonn, Germany.

After the Taliban abandoned Kabul, some Americans became giddy about the easy victory. Afghanistan made it three straight wars—after Bosnia and Kosovo—in which U.S. troops had participated without suffering a single combat fatality. It seemed that the United States had stumbled onto a new form of warfare, perhaps one perfectly tailored for the twenty-first century. It involved devastating U.S. air power combined with a few specialists on the ground and "proxy" troops who would do the actual fighting. U.S. military casualties were thus unnecessary. With America now fully engaged in southern Asia, hawks were clamoring to expand the war by next attacking Iraq. Though Iraq had not been involved in the September 11 attacks, many in the Bush administration still held a grudge against Saddam Hussein for surviving the Gulf War and because of evidence he was building weapons of mass destruction. Clinton's former adviser, Dick Morris, was prominent among those advocating that the U.S. repeat its new formula of warfare by using Shi'ites in the south and Kurds in the north of Iraq as proxy troops in the next round.

Other Americans were displeased that Northern Alliance rather than U.S. soldiers were achieving the ground victory in Afghanistan. Though it was clear that Afghanistan was not a proper environment for heavy armor, many wondered what had become of legendary American formations such as the U.S. Marines, the 82nd and 101st Airborne Divisions, the 10th Mountain Division, or light elements of the 1st Infantry Division, the "Big Red One"? If September 11 had not provided the U.S. Army and Marines impetus enough to fight, what contingency would?

The situation around Kunduz had meanwhile turned messy. It was apparent that many of the Taliban wanted to surrender, but Arabs and other diehard foreign volunteers were preventing them. Rumors came in that Arabs were shooting Taliban Pashtuns in the city to prevent them from defecting. U.S. B-52s and fighter bombers plastered Taliban positions in and around the town. During the two-week siege, Northern Alliance troops reported a stream of Pakistani aircraft flying into Kunduz's airfield at night, taking their nationals to safety. Convoys of pickup trucks packed with Taliban meanwhile flowed south from Kunduz, Northern Alliance troops chasing them with occasional fire while basically letting them go. On November 24, Western journalists recorded the astonishing scene of about seven hundred Afghan Taliban emerging from the city waving and smiling in response to Northern Alliance cheers, even shaking hands with their besiegers. In contrast, some four hundred non-Afghan fighters—mostly Pakistani but including Arabs and others—were taken prisoner by Dostum and placed in a large nineteenth-century fortress called Qala Jangi near Mazar.

Kunduz fell on the twenty-sixth as Dostum's Uzbek troops roamed the streets killing last-ditch holdouts. . . .

Toward a New Government

In early December, the council of Afghan leaders in Bonn agreed to name Hamid Karzai, a Durrani Pashtun, head of an interim government. Rabbani, the political head of the Northern Alliance, stood aside, though with a profound silence that bordered on ominous. The interim government was nevertheless packed with Tajiks and other Northern Alliance representatives as heads of defense, intelligence, interior, and other important posts. . . .

While the U.S. pondered the problem of forming a proxy "Southern Alliance" that could match the achievements of the Northern one, Kandahar was abandoned by the Taliban on December 7. The Taliban capital thus fell exactly two months after American air strikes had begun and before any U.S. ground troops could get started. The city fell to two quarreling factions of Pashtuns who fired at each other in the process. Two days later, the last vestige of Taliban rule in Afghanistan disappeared when the province of Zabul, on the Pakistani border, surrendered.

The sudden collapse of the Taliban came as a surprise. It appeared, in fact, that for several years the Taliban regime had successfully concealed from the entire world its true fragility. The fierce rhetoric and fiery dedication of its leaders had disguised the fact that it sat on shaky ground, having instituted not only a politically autocratic but restrictive theocratic regime upon a country that was not accustomed to government rule at all. The withdrawal of Pakistani support was a major factor in its demise, as was the arrival of U.S. air power, blasting Taliban troops, installations, and convoys wherever they could be found. But the movement was primarily overthrown by the Afghans themselves. At one point the Taliban had been welcomed as a surprising solution that retrieved the country from anarchy, but its notion of order was not followed by skill at government. By 2001 most Afghans had become tired of the fanaticism, and when the country became the focus of the entire world's attention after September 11, the native population espied possible new hopes for the future.

Pakistan May Have Supported the Taliban and International Terrorists

By Elizabeth Rubin

In October 2002 the United States joined forces with an Afghan military faction known as the Northern Alliance in an attempt to depose the Taliban, which controlled most of the country. Although Pakistan lent its support to the effort, many commentators questioned that nation's commitment to the cause. Many of the Taliban had studied in madrassas, or religious schools, in Pakistan. In the following article, Elizabeth Rubin, who covered the U.S.-led war against the Taliban for The New Republic *magazine, describes her encounters with the Northern Alliance soldiers. Rubin recounts the belief, held by many of the Alliance soldiers, that the Taliban, as well as international terrorists, were directly supported by Pakistan.*

Yesterday, in A field encircled by willow trees and surrounded by close to a thousand men of all ages, a dozen whip-wielding horsemen cantered around and into each other, grabbing after the carcass of a headless goat. A burly man in knee-high sheepskin boots, baggy woolen trousers, and a thick, black wool cardigan that barely stretched over his shoulders, hunched over the headless sack of goat he'd hitched between his horse's belly and his stirrup and managed to gallop to the edge of the playground, around a flag post, and back into center field

Elizabeth Rubin, "Playing Games," *The New Republic*, November 5, 2001, pp. 26–29. Copyright © 2001 by *The New Republic*. Reproduced by permission.

to bulldoze his wild, dusty white horse through the others and drop the goat into one of the two pits that serve as goalposts.

The man was Nour Habib, commander of the town of Gulbahar. His horse is one of the best, worth $15,000, but not for sale. And the game is *buzkushi*, a kind of Afghan polo. It's thrilling and dizzying to watch. The men, their horses, the colored saddles, and whips are shrouded in swirling dust. Often you can't tell whether there are any teams or rules, which is why the game is frequently used to describe the politics of the ethnic Uzbeks. They're a Turkic people, mostly in northern Afghanistan, whose commander, Rashid Dostum, a rich, womanizing, old-time warlord, infamous for allegiance-swapping, is now in a pitched battle to wrest the northern town of Mazar-e-Sharif from the Taliban. The United States is supposedly helping him do that. But, for the past week, Northern Alliance commanders here—both north of Gulbahar, in the Panjshir Valley, and south in Parwan province around Kabul—have felt like they're inside a Buzkushi dust cloud, bewildered by America's military and political aims.

As the horses rolled around, scratching their backs in the dusty pits during a recess, Commander Habib said that the game was a good way of relaxing his men. "It's good for their morale," he told his audience under the boiling mid-morning sun. "It helps dissipate their anger and aggression." Since the U.S. military campaign began [on October 7, 2001], commanders have been awaiting permission to retake Kabul, the ultimate prize. "If it were my decision I'd go to Kabul in an hour, but the decision is with our leaders," said Habib. But listening to the Dari-language BBC, or Iranian radio, or Voice of America in Persian, they've discovered that even their leaders are not calling the shots anymore. To them, once again, Afghan soil has become the staging ground for external imperial battles.

Meanwhile the soldiers wait. One evening I visited a command base for a mountain range northwest of Kabul. We walked up the sandy slopes followed by trails of children. A crimson sun set behind the range. In a cleft in the hills, I met a field commander and his young men—all of them welcoming and undyingly dedicated. Through their high-resolution binoculars, they pointed out tiny, robed Taliban soldiers, in silhouette against the night sky, climbing up and down a distant mountain ridge. A little further south, across the Bagram airfield about 35 miles north of the capital, every night this past week you could watch dozens of Taliban pickups moving supplies and men to the front line. Yet U.S. planes were nowhere in sight. Why, the commander asked, is America bombing Kabul and not the front lines?

It was something of a rhetorical question. It's well known that, since the beginning of the war, Pakistan has been pressuring the United

States to avoid bombing frontline Taliban troops in order to prevent the Northern Alliance from marching on Kabul. What the commander really wanted to know is why the United States still supports Pakistan when everyone, he said, knows that Pakistan is the source of both the Taliban and international terrorism? Why didn't the United States bomb the terrorist training camps in Pakistan a long time ago or stop its *madrassas* from pouring out new Taliban fighters? "We're such a poor, destroyed country, that there are no real consequences for bombing us. It's cheap," the commander complained. "But if America really wants to get rid of terrorism in this region she's going to have face Pakistan." Everywhere I turned up this last week, the sentiment was nearly the same.

Northern Alliance Sentiment Toward Pakistan

On Friday afternoon, the Muslim Sabbath, hundreds of Panjshir mujahedin packed in two Russian-made military trucks were stuck on a bridge in the Gulbahar, at the southern end of the Panjshir Valley, waiting for a train of donkeys laden with straw to pass. En route to the front, fighters cheered themselves on by shouting to the men in the nearby teahouses and bazaar: "Long Live Islam. Down with Pakistan." To Western ears, these calls are a confusing muddle of allegiances and fractures. But to Afghan eyes, it is America's relationship with Pakistan that appears Byzantine and ruthlessly self-interested.

That became even more obvious the next morning, when an instructor at the military academy in Jabal Saraj addressed a thousand Northern Alliance reservists on a field littered with dead Soviet tanks. Their General Fahim, he told them, was on a tour of foreign countries. An Islamic council of 60 leaders from the Northern Alliance and 60 from the exiled King of Afghanistan's party would meet in Tashkent to decide on the future government of Afghanistan. Then he added: "Pakistan is the source of terrorism. Pakistan created the Taliban. Pakistan supported Osama bin Laden. And the president of Pakistan told the U.S. Secretary of State Colin Powell that the Northern Alliance should not be part of the future government of Afghanistan. We must fight not only with terrorists but with the supporters of terrorism." The crowd cried out on cue: "Long Live Islam! Down With Pakistan!"

And I heard the refrain yet again on a visit to another Northern Alliance leader, General Anwari. His office in Gulbahar is a two-story building perched over a river and overlooking a car mechanic's junkyard, equipped with satellite phones and a small black-and-white Sanyo television that was showing an old BBC documentary of the mujahedin struggle against the Soviets. Anwari is the leader of the Harakat-i-Islami, a Shia party of the ethnic Hazara, who come from the Hazarajat, the central provinces in the Hindu Kush [mountains of Northern Afghanistan]. The Hazara's Mongol features, it is said, are the result of intermarriage between the warriors of Genghis Khan and the indigenous Tajik and Turkic peoples. The Hazara have suffered ruthless massacres at the hands of the Taliban. Fingering his yellow prayer beads, Anwari's deputy said, "After the attack in New York and D.C., the U.S. put pressure on Pakistan not to support the Taliban, and so they've created an open-minded Taliban." Is America that naïve, he wondered? There is no such thing as a Taliban who is open-minded or moderate. As my translator, an engineering student from Kabul, added, Taliban means student, but it also implies close-minded.

We had heard this before, and were going into a near coma from the propaganda and the heat, when suddenly an elderly man with Asian eyes and a wild laugh bounced into headquarters to see the general. He was, of all things, a professor of molecular biology, dressed in a black velvet blazer, a twill Scottish cap, and silk argyle socks. Speaking to me in English, Professor Ali kept referring to the unwitting men in our company as "those other fundamentalists." ("I bet they won't shake your hand," he said to me several times.) "I describe them as living in a vestigial state of evolution," he added with a howl. "It's fun to tease and fight them. They are just suckers and so boring. Aren't they?" he asked. "Admit it, I'm the first person today who's spoken to you honestly, no? We are completely beset in this country by extremists on all sides."

The professor lived and studied in Boulder, Colorado, for twelve years but, when he returned to visit his family in 1982, the Communist regime in Kabul wouldn't let him go back, so he headed up the medical faculty there. Later, when the Taliban stormed Kabul, he fled to Mazar-e-Sharif, where he established another medical faculty. Still, even the worldly professor knew who the enemy was. Whenever the satellite phone rang or the other men in the room fell into a discussion, he would lean over and whisper about Pakistan. "I am quite sure they are cheating your government," he said. "They know where Mullah Omar and bin Laden are. The ISI [the Pakistani Inter-Services Intelligence] knows every single hideout in this country, but they'll never tell."

The next day, at the professor's insistence, we stopped by his university office near the new airport being built for the Northern Alliance. There he pulled out a map and began drawing circles with his finger. "There it is," he said. "It's one of only two places he could be hiding." He was talking about bin Laden. The region was called

Shahristan, in the southern province of Uruzgan, where Mullah Omar was born, a region of high, inaccessible mountains with hundreds of caves—about 34 degrees by 67 degrees on a specialized map. The professor said he'd received information from his former medical students that they'd spotted bin Laden there 15 days earlier. "I read that five million dollars is the reward for people who offer information on his whereabouts. I could have gotten it but I was scared for my family. So now I'm telling you," he said.

There is, of course, history behind this hatred. The Taliban's primary recruiting grounds were the *madrassas* of Pakistan—in particular, the *madrassa* of Samiul Haq, a religious leader who has been a member of the Pakistan National Assembly and a senator. His *madrassa*, Dar-ul-Uloom Haqqania, graduated at least eight Taliban cabinet ministers and dozens of Taliban governors, military commanders, judges, and bureaucrats. Located on the Islamabad-Peshawar highway, it has a boarding school for 1,500, a high school for 1,000 day students, and twelve smaller *madrassas.* As Ahmed Rashid, author of *Taliban*, has written, in February of 1999 it was the most popular *madrassa* in northern Pakistan. Haq sets aside at least 400 places for Afghans and 60 more for students from Tajikistan. Uzbekistan, and Kazakhstan, often members of the radical Islamic opposition.

"Haq is in constant touch with [Mullah] Omar, helps him deal with international relations and offers advice on important Sharia decisions," writes Rashid. "He is also the principle [sic] organizer for recruiting Pakistani students to fight for the Taliban." In 1997, Rashid writes, Omar asked Haq for help in the battle for the city of Mazar-e-Sharif. "[Haq] sent his entire student body to fight alongside the Taliban." The following year, through Haq's negotiations, a number of local schools shut down for one month and sent 8,000 students to Afghanistan. This support, writes Rashid, a journalist in Lahore and one of the most knowledgeable sources on the Taliban, is separate from the regular reinforcements the Taliban receive from Pakistan's government, its established Islamic organizations, and its intelligence services.

Interrogation of a Captive Talib

Over the weekend I drove back into the Panjshir Valley, where the river runs fast and autumn is in full swing, to the Northern Alliance's Ministry of Justice prison not far from where [the Afghan general] Ahmad Shah Massoud lived. There are a few soldiers posted on the mud-brick square complex, but security is based largely on the prison's inaccessibility: To reach it you must wade through the river and then cross a suspension bridge made of narrow sheets of metal. Daily life for the prisoners mimics the *madrassa* schedule they followed in Pakistan, which is where most of them come from. They sleep 25 to a room, their narrow mattresses lined up side by side. From the log rafters, they hang their belongings: Adidas sacks, plastic bags, tea kettles, blackened cooking pans, bloodied beef bones on a string. They stack Korans of every size on small shelves. They wake up before sunrise for ablutions [ritual washing] and morning prayer. The rest of the day is parceled out between fetching water, Koranic study, prayer, and meals.

The director—a doctor, comedian, and propaganda artist—brought in a slew of prisoners. They've all been detained for between two and five years. They have no radio, televisions, or magazines and, had journalists not begun showing up at the prison, they never would have known what has happened over the past six weeks. The first man we met was Faqir Mohammad Darwesh, who started his fighting, at 15, against the Russians. He had only had three years of school and said he couldn't read or write. He had one glass eye, permanently wide open with the bottom eyelid sagging, a full beard, a mustache, and robes. He'd met Mullah Omar when Omar was a commander with the Islamic Movement based in Pakistan. Yes, he said without inflection, the attacks on the World Trade Center and the Pentagon were good because they were done in the name of Allah. If any Muslims died there, that's OK: They were worshipping money and they'll go to Allah anyway. He'd vaguely heard of Osama bin Laden and thought he might be a terrorist but didn't know much about him.

Much stranger was Saluddin Khalid, a young prisoner with hyperthyroid eyes, plastic glasses, a long beard, dark skin, and brown long robes who, it was said, came from Pakistan. He sat forward on the balls of his feet and said very quickly in English: "I am a member of a fundamentalist organization called Harikat Islam. I was fighting in Khost province for two years and then in Kashmir for a year, and then I came back to Afghanistan." Then, after my translator left the room, he said very fast. "Everything I'm telling you is a lie. My real interview was taken by the International Red Cross. The number is 31930. I was a Sunni Muslim from Iran working against the government, and I escaped to Pakistan, where I became an Islamic master writing for the Islamic magazine. Because I was Persian they sent me to Kabul and I was surrounded by them. I hid my ID because I thought their connection with Iran was too good and they'd send me back. I never imagined they'd arrest me if I said I was from Pakistan. First they made me into an officer of the Pakistani intelligence services [ISI] and after a year I had to dish out this Islamic fundamentalist line, that I want to control Afghanistan."

At that moment my translator returned, and Khalid began again: "I am happy about the attacks in New York and D.C. America helps Israel with three billion dollars in aid to kill Muslims. We will continue our fighting in Pakistan and America with our secret cells and fight against the enemies of Islam." At first I believed him. But Daud, my translator, didn't believe the story, noting that Khalid's accent seemed Pakistani. He was, he surmised, probably a Pakistani changing his story to discredit the Northern Alliance.

Then there was Abdul Ghalid from Xingyang province in China. A thin man with a goatee and white skullcap, Abdul had first gone to live with relatives in Pakistan. In the late 1990s he then went to Kabul, where he attended an Islamic school for free, with a stipend from the government. There he learned not only the tenets of Taliban fundamentalism but also a modicum of military training and terrorist tactics. Had he not been caught, he almost certainly would have returned to China to ignite a separatist movement with his newly learned skills.

CHAPTER 2

Post-Taliban Afghanistan: Reconstruction and Nation Building

The United States and Afghanistan Must Work Together for Stability in Afghanistan

By George W. Bush and Hamid Karzai

After the defeat of the Taliban and the signing of the Bonn Agreement, the United States was eager to help the devastated country of Afghanistan. In January 2002 President George W. Bush and the chairman of the Afghan interim government, Hamid Karzai, met in Washington, D.C., to discuss what role the United States would play in rebuilding Afghanistan. The following statement briefly outlines not only the extent of the economic, political, and military aid the United States would be expected to provide the interim Afghan government but also expresses the mutual desire of the two countries to prevent Afghanistan from becoming a training ground for terrorists ever again.

President Bush and Chairman Karzai commit to build a lasting partnership for the 21st century, determined to fight terrorism, and ensure security, stability and reconstruction for Afghanistan, and foster representative and accountable government for all Afghan women and men.

We stand together for a new and better future for Afghanistan—a future free from terror, war, and want. We pledge our respect for the culture and traditions of the different peoples of Afghanistan, and for the great religion of Islam, which has been tragically distorted and misused by the Taliban.

George W. Bush and Hamid Karzai, "Joint Statement on New Partnership Between U.S. and Afghanistan," The White House Online, www.whitehouse.gov, January 2002.

We reaffirm our commitment to continue to work together to rout out the remnants of the Taliban and Al Qaida network. The United States and Afghanistan stand united in our determination that Afghanistan will never again become a training ground for global terror. We are equally determined that Afghanistan's tragic experience— where terrorists were allowed to hold an entire nation hostage—will not be repeated or replicated anywhere in the world.

The United States and Afghanistan share the belief that a secure, stable Afghanistan, at peace with its neighbors, is critical to achieving our shared goals. We agree that a lasting, permanent solution for Afghanistan's security needs must be based on strengthening Afghanistan's own capacities.

We agree that the United States will work with Afghanistan's friends in the international community to help Afghanistan stand up and train a national military and police, as well as address Afghanistan's short-term security needs, including through demining assistance.

We further agree to continue to support the mission of the International Security Assistance Force (ISAF) to help promote security in Afghanistan. Chairman Karzai asked President Bush, on behalf of the Afghan people to consider supporting an extension and expansion of the ISAF.

Recognizing that representative and accountable national government is vital for Afghanistan to achieve stability, national reconciliation, and reconstruction, we reaffirm our shared determination to support the Bonn Agreement for a political transition process in Afghanistan over the next two years. Both sides recognize the importance of adhering strictly to the agreement's timetable.

We agree to support collaborative programs to strengthen Afghan civic institutions, working through Afghan and American NGOs [nongovernmental organizations] to build and strengthen political structures, independent media, human rights protections, labor unions, accountability and anti-corruption initiatives.

We also agree to launch a joint U.S.-Afghanistan Women's Council to promote private/public partnerships and mobilize resources to ensure women can gain the skills and education deprived them under years of Taliban mis-rule.

The United States and Afghanistan further agree that the Voice of America will expand its broadcast of Afghan news throughout Afghanistan as VOA and international partners work with Afghanistan to develop its own media capacity.

We both welcome the role of the United States in helping with Afghanistan's reconstruction, including the initial American contribution of nearly $297 million for Afghanistan's critical reconstruction and the transfer of $223 million in previously frozen Afghan assets.

We affirm our determination to move quickly to help Afghanistan create jobs and start rebuilding Afghanistan's agricultural sector, its health care and educational systems. Concrete examples of programs, in addition to our current humanitarian aid program and contributions to large infrastructure projects, that will have immediate impact are to:

• print and distribute nearly 10 million textbooks in Dari and Pashtu, focused on math, reading and science, in time for the official start of the Afghan school year in March;

• provide basic training for 4,000 teachers, at least half of whom are women;

• vaccinate 2.2 million Afghan children against measles and set up primary care community health clinics; and

• use $45 million in food-related programs to, in part, promote recovery by providing food directly to teachers and students at school and food to workers at project sites.

Our joint commitment to the development of Afghanistan's private sector will be bolstered by an initial U.S. Overseas Private Investment Corporation (OPIC) $50 million line of credit to finance qualified U.S. private sector projects.

We are pleased to announce that in February [2002] OPIC [the Overseas Private Investment Company], the Export-Import Bank, and the U.S. Trade Development Agency, will conduct an investment assessment mission to Afghanistan and that the Commerce Department will lead a private sector mission to Afghanistan to help identify Afghanistan's investment needs and opportunities for U.S. private sector participation in reconstruction.

We welcome a U.S. Department of Labor initiative to fund job generation and training programs for ex-combatants and women.

Finally, we pledge to enhance understanding between the citizens of our two countries by promoting people-to-people exchanges and cultural initiatives, including through the Fulbright, International Visitor and Humphrey programs, as well as through non-governmental organizations.

Recognizing that the Taliban destroyed several of Afghanistan's great historic statues and cultural sites, we agreed to work together to help restore and preserve Afghanistan's heritage.

Afghanistan's Interim Government Is Flawed

By Larry P. Goodson

After the fall of the Taliban, Afghanistan was left without a governing body. In December 2001 a delegation of Afghan diplomats and refugees arrived in Bonn, Germany, to create the parameters of a provisional Afghan government. Then, in June 2002, a loya jirga, *or grand assembly, was convened in Afghanistan in order to put together an interim government. Larry P. Goodson, an associate professor of international studies at Bentley College in Waltham, Massachusetts, writes that the* loya jirga *process was, by and large, a failure. As evidence, he notes that several warlords who have been chief proponents of war and instability in the country for years, and who carry with them unresolved tribal rivalries, now occupy high positions in the interim government.*

I had already been in Afghanistan for four weeks and on the eve of the Grand Assembly, or Loya Jirga, convened in mid-June 2002 to elect a transitional government, I realized it would be a failure.

For almost two months, district and provincial elections had occurred all over the country to select delegates to attend the Assembly at Kabul Polytechnic University. Afghan election teams, assisted by staff from the United Nations and a handful of international monitors, of whom I was one, worked hard and with some degree of success to ensure that the powerful warlords of Afghanistan would not control the outcome.

Larry P. Goodson, "Inside Afghanistan: A Failed Opportunity," *Newsday*, July 21, 2002. Copyright © 2002 by Newsday, Inc. Reproduced by permission of the author.

Yet, to my dismay, as I sweltered in the registration tent two days before the Loya Jirga began, helping to process the incoming delegates, I saw more and more of the people we had tried to keep out. Warlords, drug lords, provincial governors and their entourages; suddenly the little guys were being crowded out by powerful last-minute appointees who were given free passes to ensure that Hamid Karzai would be elected head of state, and that government by warlord would continue. When the Assembly concluded, the interim government of the previous six months was returned to power essentially unchanged.

It was a missed opportunity for a big step toward democracy and reconstruction, which would provide the foundation for stability in post-Taliban Afghanistan. America's first battle against terrorism has displaced a murderous regime but left behind a highly unstable replacement and a good deal of swelling anger among the ethnically divided population. This combination could end up breeding even more anti-Western terrorists.

In the streets of Kabul, you can see the tension, such as when the police force staged a one-day walkout in protest at the appointment of a new interior minister of a different ethnic group than most of the officers.

What Went Wrong?

The first problem is that the country has a new government led by a member of the dominant Pushtun ethnic group but controlled by the northern minorities, which has many Pushtuns seething. The deposed Taliban were largely a Pushtun movement, and the Pushtuns are paying the price for backing the wrong horse prior to Sept. 11, 2001, even though most of their people, or even the Taliban themselves, knew nothing of the planned attacks on the United States.

The Northern Alliance, which the United States supported in military operations to overthrow the Taliban in late 2001, was composed primarily of Tajiks, Hazaras and Uzbeks. The Pushtuns have controlled Afghanistan for virtually all its modern history and are chafing under a government dominated by the "Panjshiri mafia," a term that refers to the power of three Tajik warlords from the Panjshir Valley northeast of Kabul—new Vice President and Defense Minister Mohammad Fahim, Foreign Minister Abdullah Abdullah and former Interior Minister and new Education Minister Yunus Qanooni.

The Pushtuns are the world's largest remaining tribal people, and are divided and sub-divided into numerous tribes, clans and sub-clans. The main two divisions are between southern Pushtuns, the group to which both Hamid Karzai and former king Zahir Shah belong, and eastern Pushtuns, the group to which recently assassinated Vice President and Public Works Minister Haji Abdul Qadir belonged.

It is no surprise that rumors in Kabul place the blame for Qadir's assassination on the Panjshiris, although Qadir's many local enemies from his days as a warlord and drug smuggler also provide suspects, as do frustrated southern Pushtuns linked with the Taliban.

Even more exasperating than the tribal tensions coming out of the Loya Jirga is the fact that this failed opportunity was due at least in part to bad policymaking by the UN and U.S. chiefs in Kabul. Lakhdar Brahimi, the special representative of the UN Secretary General, insisted that the UN have only a "light footprint" in Afghanistan's political reconstruction—with a minimal presence of soldiers and observers—when much heavier involvement is required to force the warlords to cede power to a national government.

The United States is also guilty, but of a clumsy footprint, both through its political mishandling of the formation of the new government and its military mistakes such as the tragic bombing deaths of civilians [in July of 2002] in Uruzgan.

The Policy Makers

The two chief architects of U.S policy in Afghanistan over the past few months have been Zalmay Khalilzad and Ashraf Ghani, both Afghan-Americans. Khalilzad is a veteran of Republican administrations and senior National Security Council staff member that President George W. Bush made his special envoy to Afghanistan, while Ghani is a one-time World Bank staffer and anthropologist at Johns Hopkins University who returned to Afghanistan after Sept. 11 and became an adviser to Karzai. Both were credited with substantial behind-the-scenes roles by knowledgeable sources in Kabul during and prior to the Loya Jirga, and both were not averse to more public roles as it went on.

Khalilzad addressed informal gatherings of delegates to push for Karzai's leadership, and appeared to play a key role in persuading elderly former king Zahir Shah to throw his support to Karzai, effectively scuttling the effort to restore the monarchy that had widespread support among the Loya Jirga delegates.

Ghani was often seen taking second-tier ministers on "power strolls" behind the big tent where they could press their cases to be considered in the new cabinet, and ended the Loya Jirga as Karzai's powerful new Finance Minister. Both of these men have deep knowledge of Afghanistan and a passion to rebuild the country, but both have ties to players within Afghan politics, and may find their policy positions caught between what Washington wants and what their Afghan friends want.

At the very least, their roles have left the United States with an uncertain chain-of-command in Kabul (which must be especially frustrating for the nominal U.S. chief there, veteran diplomat Ambassador Robert Finn). This makes it very difficult to discern whether America's Afghan policy is being directed from the White House, the State Department or the Defense Department, and precisely what the policy is.

What Must Be Done

What is required in the ongoing rebuilding of the Afghan nation is to tie the Pushtuns to this Tajik-dominated Kabul government, but the Pushtuns will not put up with a non-democratic government dominated by the northern minorities for very long. They will for now, since the United States and coalition military presence in Kandahar and Afghan airspace prevents any serious challenge to the status quo, but that could change when outside military forces leave.

I made just this point to a senior American diplomat in Kabul, arguing that the one thing that the Loya Jirga had to produce was some greater role for the currently marginalized Pushtuns; I was given the party line that the Pushtun leaders (except Karzai) have too much drug money or blood on their hands. But that's true for many leading figures in the current regime as well. Afghanistan has been the world's leading producer of heroin in recent years, and both Taliban and the Northern Alliance commanders were involved in the trade.

Another troublesome sign is the return to prominence, as senior advisers, of northern power-brokers like ex-President Burhanuddin Rabbani and warlord theologian Abdul Rasoul Sayyaf, both of whom have strong Islamic fundamentalist credentials and wish to push the new government toward Taliban-like social policies. Perhaps ominously, only one female was appointed to Karzai's new cabinet, and the Ministry of Women's Affairs was dropped.

As the talk in Washington turns increasingly to Iraq, Afghanistan remains a powerful object lesson about U.S. policy in the post- Sept. 11 world. America's failure to capture or kill either Osama bin Laden or Taliban leader Mohammad Omar raises doubts about any strategy built on capturing or eliminating Saddam Hussein. And this country's inability to broker a broader-based government or a more democratic system in Afghanistan should make Americans think twice about what kind of government and social conditions might follow Saddam's overthrow, were it to occur.

The International Community Should Not Attempt to Impose Democracy on Afghanistan

By Marina Ottaway and Anatol Lieven

Experts debate how to approach the reconstruction of Afghanistan to create a stable state after the fall of the Taliban. Marina Ottaway and Anatol Lieven, senior associates at the Carnegie Endowment for International Peace, contend in the following article that, despite its best wishes and intentions, the international community should not expect the creation of a modern democratic state in Afghanistan. Instead, the authors argue, Western nations should acknowledge the influence that warlords have on the shaping of Afghan politics and should strive, through the means of the UN and a sustained international military effort, to ensure basic stability and security, and a possibility for trade in Afghanistan.

A fghanistan after the Taliban may easily turn into a quagmire for the international community, and the wrong kind of international strategies may easily worsen both its problems and America's. In particular, to begin with a grossly over-ambitious program of reconstruction risks acute disillusionment, international withdrawal, and a plunge into a new cycle of civil war and religious fanaticism.

Ambitious plans to turn this war-hardened, economically ravaged, deeply divided country into a modern democratic state are being pro-

Marina Ottaway and Anatol Lieven, "Rebuilding Afghanistan," *Current History*, vol. 101, March 2002, pp. 133–38. Copyright © 2002 by Carnegie Endowment for International Peace. Reproduced with permission.

posed and have even been incorporated into the December 5, 2001 Bonn agreement among Afghan leaders. But nobody is proposing the full-fledged, long-term military occupation that would be required even to attempt such a transformation—one reason being that past occupations, whether British or Soviet, have ended in utter disaster. At most, the international community is speaking of a relatively lightly armed presence in Kabul [the Afghan capital] and certain other centers.

The chances of successfully imposing effective modern democratic state structures on Afghanistan thus are negligible. Even with a massive Western military presence on the ground, the West has already run into serious problems in transforming tiny Bosnia. Afghanistan is a country 12 times the size of Bosnia with 26 million people; an extremely difficult terrain; an ethnically, tribally, and religiously segmented society; and a fearsome array of battle-hardened warlords who have no good reason to give up their power.

But the world cannot afford to turn its back on Afghanistan in frustration, as it has done in the past, lest the country again become a haven for terrorists and an international threat. Afghanistan needs a modest reconstruction program that does not require full-fledged military occupation and is tailored to the reality of the country.

A Century of Troubled State Building

The Afghan state is a recent, partly colonial creation that has never commanded the full loyalty of its own citizens. Even today, many—perhaps most—Afghans give their primary allegiance to local leaders, ethnic groups, and tribes.

Afghanistan was only created at the end of the nineteenth century. All of its borders were determined by the British Empire, and reflected not an internal historical or ethnic logic, but an imperial one. Its northern border marked the furthest extent to which Britain was prepared to see the Russian empire advance. Its southern and eastern borders were the furthest limit to which the British Indian Empire felt it necessary and safe to extend itself. Within these borders an Afghan state with modern trappings was created by a confluence of British geopolitical interest and the ruthless government of King Abdur Rahman, the so-called Iron Amir, who reigned from 1880 to 1901. The king was a highly competent ruler who, by quite fiendish methods and with massive subsidies of money and weapons from the British, created the basis—albeit limited—for a centralized Afghan state.

Abdur Rahman's reign marked the start of the Afghan state-building process. In Europe, this process began in the early Middle Ages, stretched over several centuries with numerous catastrophic setbacks, and was attended by immense cruelty, resistance, and devastation. It therefore is hardly surprising that the very short Afghan state-building process met fierce resistance, had limited success, and ultimately collapsed—especially given the intensely warlike, independent, and anarchic traditions of many Afghan peoples, including the largest ethnos, the Pashtuns.

Abdur Rahman laid the foundations not only for the centralizing and modernizing Afghan state, but also for the alienation from that state of the religious, tribal, and ethnic groups that dominate Afghan society. This alienation helped bring about the failure of the Afghan constitutional monarchy in the 1960s and early 1970s and tore the country apart in the following decades.

Had the modern Afghan state succeeded in developing Afghanistan and bringing visible benefits to the mass of the population, hostility to the state would gradually have faded. But, as with state building in so much of the world, it failed to do so, and its one area of partial success helped seal its own fate. The modern education system, although limited to a small fraction of the population (and of course an even smaller proportion of women), created a mass of educated graduates and junior bureaucrats and military officers for whom no well-paying jobs could be found either in the impoverished private sector or state service. Their bitter frustration produced the communist revolution of 1978, which essentially was an attempt to relaunch the state's modernizing program in an ultraradical guise by returning to Abdur Rahman's savage methods.

The communists' program, like that of Abdur Rahman, depended critically on subsidies and weapons from an outside protector, in this case the Soviet Union. And as in the Iron Amir's time, this foreign support helped spark fierce resistance from a variety of religious, ethnic, and tribal groups. The resistance eventually triumphed, and between 1978 and 1992 it overthrew the communist regime and eventually the Afghan state itself, first in the mountains, then across most of the country, and finally in Kabul and the other main cities. Tragically, but not surprisingly, the resistance proved completely incapable of replacing this state with any unified authority of its own, except—after a period of violent chaos—in the pathological and temporary form of the Taliban.

The difficulty of creating an Afghan state based on anything but sheer coercion has been immensely complicated by the region's ethnic makeup. The original "state-forming" ethnic group, the Pashtuns, make up less than half the total population, with the rest divided among a wide range of different nationalities. Tajiks, Uzbeks, and Hazaras (Shias of Mongolian descent) are the largest groups and are mentioned most often, but several smaller ones play key roles in their own areas.

Equally important, the Pashtuns' own role in the history of the modern Afghan state has been profoundly ambiguous. Afghanistan is a Pashtun creation, achieved through a Pashtun dynasty, and to this day the Pashtuns constitute the core of the country. But Pashtun tribal society is highly segmented and thus radically unfit to serve as the basis for the formation of a unitary state. Pashtun and other tribal revolts against the state's modernizing policies, often led by local religious figures, plagued all Afghan rulers. They played a central part in the rebellion against communist rule, and in the general reaction against Western modernity and modern state institutions that followed.

The Choices

In the past several decades, the international community has relied on three approaches to deal with countries that descend into chaos. It has supported strongmen capable of reimposing order by force; it has given up in despair, leaving the country to sort out its problems as best it can; and, most recently; it has embarked on ambitious projects to reconstruct the country in the image of a modern secular, multiethnic, and democratic state. None of these approaches should be used in Afghanistan, but something can be learned from each of them.

A compromise approach needs to be based on an awareness both of Afghanistan's past and its present conditions, not on an image of the modern state the West would like it to become. The international community must recognize that in the northern half of the country, the coherence of the Northern Alliance is unlikely to last for long without its raison d'être [reason for existence] of resistance to the Taliban, whereas in the Pashtun areas confusion reigns. In short, it will be extremely difficult to create any unifying political structures.

Heavily armed tribal groups will not surrender their arms or their local power unless they are forced to do so by a national government with a powerful army of its own or by an overwhelming outside force. Because the international community is not prepared to produce an occupying force on the same scale as that deployed in Bosnia and Kosovo—thus, many times larger in absolute terms the democratic-reconstruction model cannot be implemented. Indeed, it would almost certainly fail even if such a force were deployed. The strategy therefore needs to be less invasive.

The now-discredited strongman model is historically the favored method to stabilize a country in crisis; it was freely employed, for instance, by the United States during the cold war and by France as part of its neocolonial strategy in Africa. It is not ethically appealing, but it is cheap, can be effective for a time, and requires little effort on the part of international actors, who delegate the job of imposing order to local leaders. There is no conceivable strongman or strong organization for Afghanistan as a whole. There are, however, strongmen controlling different regions. They will remain part of the political scene, and the international community has no choice but to work with them as it has worked with other such leaders in the past.

The Democratic-Reconstruction Model Is Inappropriate

Today's orthodox approach to restoring states is much more democratic, but also much more invasive and costly, yet not particularly successful. For the past 10 years, the explicit goal of the international community has been to transform countries in crisis into democratic states with a free market economy based on the argument that only such states benefit their citizens and safeguard the international need for stability in the long run. This Western-dominated sociopolitical engineering approach is becoming ever more complex and costly as experience reveals new areas where intervention is needed.

The components of the democratic-reconstruction model can be summarized as follows: the parties involved in the conflict must reach agreement on a new permanent political system. Elections must be held as soon as possible. The new state must be multiethnic, secular, and democratic—regardless of whether this has any basis in local tradition, or whether it is what the inhabitants of the country want. While the accord is being implemented, peace and order are guaranteed by an international force, as well as by the presence of a large number of UN administrators. The international financial institutions take on the restructuring of the country's economy. International nongovernmental organizations (NGOs) are funded to work in their specialized areas, ranging from humanitarian aid to election organizing.

Elements of the democratic-reconstruction model are already beginning to show up in the discussions of what to do in Afghanistan. The agreement reached by the Afghan factions in Bonn provides for the formation in six months of a broadly based interim government giving representation to all ethnic groups and to women, followed by elections two years later. Virtually all international organizations and NGOs demand strong action to promote women's rights. The World Bank's Afghanistan "Approach Paper" calls for helping the country to build a strong central bank and ministry of finance and for capacity building in all economic institutions. Other organizations target the strengthening of civil society. And this is only the beginning.

Not only is most of this impossible in Afghanistan today, but much of it fits only the wishes of a small minority of Westernized urban

Afghans, many of whom have spent the past generation living in the West and are out of touch with their own society. They also, consciously or unconsciously, have a vested interest in Western strategies that would guarantee maximum employment and status for themselves. The model would need to be imposed on reluctant tribal leaders and warlords, on religious authorities, and probably on most ordinary Afghans, and would thus require a strong foreign military and civilian presence, projecting to the world the image of a Muslim country under foreign occupation. As in Somalia, the outcome would almost certainly be conflict between the international force and powerful local groups.

Ordered Anarchy

This conflict would most likely lead sooner or later to a swing in exactly the opposite direction, toward withdrawal and neglect, as happened in Somalia and in Afghanistan a decade ago. The reason was the same in both cases: the countries concerned did not appear sufficiently important to justify the effort to create order. The consequences of neglect were serious. Afghanistan became a haven for Al Qaeda. Somalia spawned not only harmless homegrown and clan-based Islamist groups but also al-Itihaad al-Islamiya, an organization aligned with Al Qaeda whose operatives were involved in the 1998 attacks on the United States embassies in Kenya and Tanzania.

In Somalia, however, neglect also had some positive consequences, and this lesson must be heeded in designing a strategy for Afghanistan. With no center to be held, and no pot of foreign aid to be fought over, fighting in Somalia was greatly reduced and mechanisms were developed to compensate for the absence of the state. This did not necessarily mean reverting to a completely primitive life within villages and clans. A new class of international traders emerged, for example, who are capable of financing complex transactions, making international payments, and developing markets.

The Somali experience has historical precedents. The "ordered anarchy" of medieval France, Germany, or Italy—characterized by multiple overlapping armed authorities—did not preclude the establishment of great and stable long-range trade routes and commercial and financial networks, major economic growth, and tremendous achievements in human culture. In the long run, these also laid the foundations for the growth of a modern judicial order, which in turn was an essential basis for the economic revolution and the modern state. The international community must initially accept some version of ordered anarchy in Afghanistan and work to attenuate its worst shortcomings.

The Right Choice

The international community's immediate aim for the Afghan government should therefore not be the impossible fantasy of a democratic government technocratically administering the country, but rather the formation of a loose national mediation committee functioning not just for the initial six months but indefinitely. This committee should seek not to create the entire apparatus of a modern state, but rather the minimal conditions for medieval civilization: the avoidance of major armed conflict, the security of main trade routes, and the safety and neutrality of the capital. These conditions should be secured not by an Afghan national army—another empty fantasy, given the present situation—but by an international force created by the United Nations and backed by the ultimate sanction of American airpower. An agreement on how to create such minimal conditions would be a greater accomplishment for the *loya jirga* [grand assembly] called for by the Bonn agreement than would approval of a Western-style democratic constitution that could never be implemented.

Most Western aid therefore should not be directed through the Afghan government—even assuming that the appearance of a broadly based national government could be sustained—but should be provided directly to Afghanistan's regions. Aid should, moreover, be used in a quite clearheaded and tough way as an instrument of peacekeeping—as a way to give local warlords and armies an incentive not to go to war with each other. It would be a bribe of sorts, and might appear to perpetuate the power of warlords. But as Somalia and other African examples illustrate, greater risks would be involved in making the central government the chief channel for international aid, since this would make control of the government and the city of Kabul a vital goal for the country's various armed forces. Aid itself would become a source of future conflict.

Aid should also be provided directly at the local level, of course, to villages and local organizations. But the international community should have no illusion that it is possible to completely bypass warlords and tribal leaders in this fashion. In the end, as the experiences of aid agencies in many countries show, armed groups and powerful individuals always influence how aid is used in their areas.

Key Principles

The international strategy toward Afghanistan should therefore be based on these key principles:

• Discard the assessments of what help Afghanistan needs to become a modern democratic state and replace them with a sober evaluation of the minimal tasks a central administration needs to perform to allow a measure of normal life, economic activity, and, above all, trade.

• Work directly with regional leaders whose power is well established. Assign liaison officials to work with these leaders, monitor their behavior (especially their treatment of local ethnic minorities and their relations with other regions and ethnic groups), and make sure that they provide no shelter to terrorist groups.

• Instruct these liaison officials to work with international and domestic NGOs to ensure not only that they can work unhindered, but also that they do not become dangerously entangled in local politics.

• Create a corps of international civil servants to act as these liaison officials and otherwise assist Afghanistan. These officials should be paid generously in return for devoting a substantial term of service to this difficult and dangerous task and for investing in learning local languages, history, and customs; everything possible should be done to establish their position and prestige. A certain historical precedent here is provided by the British Empire's Indian Political Service, which managed—but, wisely, never tried to administer—the Pashtun tribal areas and handled relations with the Afghan monarchy.

• Give serious consideration to the standards that need to be met by local leaders in exchange for aid. Resist the temptation to impose unrealistic standards. Pick only a few battles to fight at one time. For example, make aid initially contingent on education for girls, but not on a comprehensive reform of legal or social codes governing the position of women in the family or major participation of women in administration. Incremental change is more likely to be sustainable.

• Accept that, even with checks and conditions, there will be corruption, and aid will help warlords consolidate their power and their client networks. Experience shows that corruption is inevitable whenever a country receives large amounts of aid, even if it is channeled through formal government institutions. Use aid quite consciously as a political tool to maintain peace.

• Establish certain basic national institutions in Kabul, but leave the question of a real national administration for Afghanistan for the distant future. Instead, treat the central government as a form of national mediation committee. Avoid making Kabul and the central government prizes worth fighting over.

• Create a substantial United Nations–mandated international force to ensure the security and neutrality of the city of Kabul as a place where representatives from different areas can meet and negotiate, and where basic national institutions can be created. Be prepared to maintain this force for a period of several years, at least.

• Do not pursue democratic measures, such as organizing elections, that would increase competition at the center among different warlords or ethnoreligious groups: in present circumstances such elections could not possibly lead to stable democratic institutions.

What Is Needed

The United States and the international community do not need Afghanistan to become a modern democratic state—even a united one—to protect their key interests. They require a cessation of serious armed conflict and sufficient access to all parts of the country to ensure that it will not again become a haven for international terrorist groups and a source of destabilization for its neighbors. Beyond this, America's interests and capabilities are highly limited.

If Afghanistan could be turned by fiat into a Scandinavian welfare state, well run and capable of delivering services to its population, its people surely would benefit greatly. But the international community cannot deliver such a state. At best, experience shows it can deliver institutions that conform to the appearance of the modern state, but that function inefficiently and corruptly and that generate new conflicts over control.

What the people of Afghanistan need most urgently, and the international community can help them obtain, is the cessation of war and the possibility of pursuing basic economic activities free from brutal oppression, ethnic harassment, and armed conflict. They need to be able to cultivate their fields, sell their products, go to market, send their children to school, receive basic medical care, and move freely around the country. In the long run, much more would be desirable, but the first step should simply be to reestablish a degree of normal life, even if it is not life in a modern state. Just to achieve this much will require many years of careful, concentrated effort by dedicated international workers on the ground. More ambitious state-building plans must be left for another generation, and to the Afghans themselves.

The Women of Afghanistan Face New Challenges After the Taliban Defeat

By Natasha Walter

The plight of Afghan women under the Taliban has been widely publicized. Pictures of women in burkas, garments that cover them from head to toe, and even public executions of women by the Taliban are now familiar images to the Western world. Now that the Taliban regime has fallen, women are embracing the possibilities of a new Afghanistan, but they are keenly aware that there is still a long way to go in procuring equality, peace, and safety. Natasha Walter, a regular columnist for the Independent, *a British newspaper, has written numerous articles on feminist issues. In the following article she explores the challenges women face in post-Taliban Afghanistan.*

The students are crammed on to the benches in the cavernous lecture hall of Kabul University's science faculty. Four hundred eager faces stare down at us, and 150 of them are female. A few rows from the front sits a young woman wearing a white lace scarf tucked tightly around her rosy face. Her name is Zohal Faiz Mohammed. She shakes her head, smiling, when I ask how she feels to be back at university after five years' absence. "I can't say my feelings—you can see. For the first time we can experience the university, this atmosphere. We can all study, boys and girls together."

Natasha Walter, "Barefaced Resistance," The Guardian Online, www.guardian.co.uk, July 20, 2002. Copyright © 2002 by Natasha Walter. Reproduced by permission.

That evening, Zohal invites us to have supper with her and her parents. They live in what is, by Kabul's standards, a comfortable neighbourhood, but that still means a chaotic stretch of apartment blocks with blown-out windows and walls riddled with bullet holes. While Zohal prepares the meal, we sit on cushions on the floor of the pink sitting room, talking to her parents. Suddenly Zohal rushes in, worried that we are bored, and shows off one of her most precious possessions, a video of songs from Indian films. "My father and I love these," she says eagerly.

She watches the gorgeous Aishwarya Rai dancing in a Technicolor field of dreams. "Isn't she beautiful?" As she watches the video, Zohal, in jeans and a white shirt with the sleeves rolled up, her thick black hair in a ponytail, looks younger than her 22 years.

She is determined to be young, determined to be happy, determined not to talk about politics—instead, we talk about her errant fiance and her plans for the future. After dinner, she, her mother and her cousin squabble over the arrangements for the photographs. "Don't fight!" Zohal says. "All right, do fight." "I'll be Rabbani and you can be Hekmatyar," says the photographer. Peals of laughter ring out. Those are the names of the men whose armies laid Kabul waste in the 1990s. "All you can do sometimes is laugh," says her mother, wiping her eyes with a corner of her scarf.

As we talk over dinner, I can't help thinking that Zohal's happiness feels like the uncomplicated optimism of any young woman at the start of her life. But Afghan women are not like other women, and when they sound optimistic, this is an act of determined bravery. On another day, when Zohal and I meet for tea, she talks about the past. Her face changes, loses its pink glow, and she fumbles with her fingers.

A History of Hardship

Her comfortable childhood came under siege in 1992, after the Soviet-backed regime fell and mujaheddin armies—armed by the west—battled for control of Kabul, street by street. "I remember every night, sitting in the corner of the room, listening to the rockets and the bombs," says Zohal in a dull tone very different from her earlier quick chatter. "And every morning we would go out and help to collect the dead bodies. There was nothing to think about. We were just waiting for our death. We had no hope for the future, not even for our lives."

Zohal's family were forced out of their home more than once when the fighting concentrated around their area. They became refugees again when they fled from the extreme oppression of the Taliban, and spent two years in Pakistan, but the destitution that faced so many Afghans there forced them back to Kabul [in 2001]. They went on the move again to the Pakistani border during the US bombing [in the winter of 2001]. Refugees three times—from the mujaheddin, the Taliban and the Americans—Zohal's family are now starting over, trying to put their lives back together out of the fragments they have left.

But Zohal's face is set towards the future. She wants to be an engineer, studies at the university in the morning, and takes English and computing classes in the afternoon. Since today is a holiday, we visit one of Kabul's newly opened beauty salons. Marya salon sits next to a restaurant where lamb kebabs are seared over open barbecues, and beside a music stall that is stacked with colourful Indian and Iranian cassettes. But even here, in this reawakened part of Kabul, if you stop on the street for a moment, the beggars, women and children, tug at your arms and hands.

Rebelling Quietly

Inside the salon, the air is thick with hairspray and scent, and Fazila, the owner, a stout woman in a black dress with neatly styled auburn hair, is getting through one client after another with astonishing speed. She and her two young daughters work like an assembly line. Curlers are whipped out and in, tweezers tug at eyebrows, kohl is rubbed on to eyelids. Shaima and Suheila, two sisters, both doctors, are waiting on Fazila's couches. Both have their hair pinned up under hairnets. Tomorrow is Shaima's wedding day and they are determined to do it in high Afghan style, all glittery dresses and curled hair and hennaed hands.

"When she had her engagement ceremony," Suheila explains, "we couldn't take photographs—though we did, secretly. We couldn't even have musicians." What would the Taliban have done if you had invited musicians? Suheila draws a finger across her throat. "But I played a cassette, quietly, and I danced—I was determined to dance." She is about to tell me more when a little boy runs in. The girls at home need more curlers. Suheila springs to her feet and picks up her burka. "Don't you want to know why I still wear this?" she asks. She stands silhouetted in the bright doorway, holding the swathe of blue nylon above her face.

The western press has made so much of the idea that, as the Taliban left Kabul, the liberated women threw off their blue shrouds. But in Kabul, almost all the young women are still wearing the burka. This is not through force of tradition. There was a custom of wearing the burka among some ethnic groups in Afghanistan, but not among educated women in the cities. I asked 20 or 30 women why they were still wearing it, and all gave the same answer. Fear.

"We aren't safe yet," says Suheila succinctly. This sense of insecurity is understandable. The mujaheddin and the Taliban weren't just a few maniacs who have now disappeared, but hundreds and thousands of "willing executioners"—men who gang-raped women as part of their wars, as the mujaheddin did, or who beat women savagely for showing their faces, as the Taliban did. These men have not gone away, and although in Kabul they are kept quiet by the presence of the international security force, if that departs, many women fear that the violence will start again.

"Of course, the burka was not the worst thing about the Taliban time," Suheila emphasises. "But until we are safe, we can't take it off." [In July 2002] reports of politically and religiously motivated violence against women continue. Human Rights Watch has documented rapes and assaults against certain ethnic groups in northern Afghanistan. Female aid workers have even been withdrawn from Mazar-i-Sharif after one was gang-raped. In Kabul [in June 2002], two women wearing scarves instead of burkas had acid sprayed in their faces. So, for the women of Afghanistan, the anonymity of the burka still gives them a sense of protection. Zohal, who also wears the burka when she goes out, agrees with Suheila.

"Of course we would like to take it off," she says, "but it just isn't possible yet."

Afghan Women Enter Politics

Some of the women who have taken off the burka are those now moving into politics. My visit coincides with the start of the loya jirga, the gathering of a council of 1,500 delegates who are to decide the structure of the future government. Nearly 200 are women. I visit the council offices, where dozens of Afghan men circle the courtyard, talking eagerly. Out on the parched grass is a tent, and inside the stifling tent sit 15 women, newly arrived delegates from western provinces of the country.

A woman in her early 30s, also called Zohal, talks enthusiastically about what this means to her. Her two-year-old daughter, silently playing with a wilted pink rose, sits on her lap as she talks. "The doors of everything have been closed to women for so long," she says. "Now we hope that the doors are swinging open. This loya jirga is only a first step, but in the future parliament there must be equal representation for women and for men."

Mindful that even in western countries women haven't achieved such representation, I ask the other women in the tent if they feel the same. There is an eruption of noise. "Yes, they all agree," my translator says solemnly. "They say that women make up more than half of the population of Afghanistan and that they have been the first victims of war. They must now be allowed their rights."

Sitting next to Zohal is Bibi Kur. . . . She comes from Herat. "There, our leaders did not want a single woman to go to the loya jirga," she says scornfully. "But people from Kabul came and insisted, so they said there could be one woman from each province, one out of eight delegates." Is she scared to be a delegate when the warlords are so against women's involvement? "I am afraid," she says. "I know these men. But I've survived 23 years of war. I have been injured.

My husband has been injured. Now I am happy that I am here and that I can defend women's rights."

It is easy to be delighted by the energy and determination of these women who are moving back into politics. But in the weeks that follow, as the loya jirga progresses, the idealistic women are sidelined. The power is still held by men who control the guns and the money, former mujaheddin who gained their influence through bloody fighting and terrorising civilians; men such as Abdul Rashid Dostum, Ismail Khan and Burhanuddin Rabbani, all of whom retain power over areas of Afghanistan and who pack the loya jirga with their supporters. Although we in the west see such men as useful allies, the women I spoke to have not forgotten their crimes. Indeed, on the first day of the loya jirga, some female delegates, among them Tajwah Kakur, confront Rabbani. "Why did your armies kill and rape so many women?" Kakur asks. "Why are there so many widows in our country?" He is silent.

Questioning Patriarchal Power

I spend an afternoon talking to Kakur at her office in the women's ministry, set up [in 2001] by the interim administration. Kakur, the deputy women's minister, sits still as a monument behind her glass-topped desk, her silver hair piled up under a grey voile scarf. She is unusual among the new women in Afghan politics, because she was even tolerated by—and herself accepted—the Taliban regime, and ran a boys' school in Kabul during their rule. Even so, she says her dreams have now come true: "I am so happy looking at women going back to work and school. I think, is this a dream? Or is it real life?"

But for all her optimistic talk, Kakur is angry about the current situation and the men who are moving back into power. "All Afghan women know who I am talking about. These men kidnapped and raped the women of Afghanistan. Until the guns are taken away from them, women will not have security. Yes, now we are told that these men are heroes. But who broke all the buildings and kidnapped the women? They are not heroes. They are zeroes."

But women in Afghanistan are not only struggling against the men who rule them. Many are simply struggling to survive. As we leave

Kakur's office, we walk through a corridor where dozens of women with their burkas pushed back from their faces are squatting outside the offices. A female official shoos them away into a courtyard. We follow them into the blinding glare of the midday sun, and ask who they are and why they are here. As they speak, I catch a glimpse of another Afghanistan, the one where so many women, especially those whose husbands and brothers were killed in the decades of fighting, now live.

One of these women, Khandijal, is five months pregnant, although her bump hardly shows on her skeletal frame, wrapped in its blue burka. Five months ago, a US bomb killed her husband and injured her leg. "For four months I have been coming here every day to beg for work," she says. "There is no work for us." Khandijal has five daughters, all younger than 12. "Every day I go back home and my children cry out, 'Where is the money, where is the food?' I have nothing for them. My children are starving and nobody here will do anything for me."

"Life for me was better under the Taliban," Hanifa, a tiny, skinny woman, says defiantly. Her husband was killed three years ago, and she has seven children. "The UN gave the widows in Kabul a card to take to a centre to get food free. We got five naan bread a day. So our children ate lunch and dinner. Now we have nothing. At first, when the Americans came, I was happy. I thought, our lives will get better. But there is nothing for us. The Americans never asked about us."

"Will you help us?" all the women ask, one by one. "Will you help to find us work?" When we explain that we don't work for the UN or an aid organisation, they look puzzled. I go on asking questions, which they answer eagerly, perhaps hoping that we will give them something in return. We have all seen and read tales of such desperation a thousand times, but looking at desperation is very different from having desperation look back at you, hungrily.

The Challenge of Humanitarian Aid

If you listen to the talk of the amount of money that has been promised to Afghanistan, it is easy to feel complacent about the way the international community is stepping in to reconstruct the country. Certainly, for many people life has improved—despite what Hanifa says, for instance, the UN World Food Programme tells me that it is now reaching about three times as many destitute people as it could under the Taliban regime. But although more aid is coming in now, far more has been promised than is reaching the country, as donors hold back in case the fragile peace collapses. And what has arrived—around $800m in the first half of the year—is not enough to stop the immediate suffering of millions of ordinary people. Afghan women are thought to have the highest maternal mortality rates of women in any country, at around 1,700 per 100,000; life expectancy is about 46 years, and around 50% of children are stunted through malnutrition—yet donor fatigue is already a real danger. Dr Lynn Amowitz of Harvard Medical School, who is leading a new maternal mortality survey in Afghanistan, said recently, "Afghanistan is falling off people's radar screen and funding is becoming harder to find."

One of the women standing with the widows is younger than they are, and her face still has the sleekness of a girl who eats every day. Akala is only 19.

"I started school again [in June 2001]," she says. "But every afternoon I come here and ask for work. There are 10 of us brothers and sisters, and my father is too old to work. For us, life is becoming worse day by day." Has she seen anything get better? "Yes, of course, we are free to go outside," she says quickly, "and now I can go to school. But what can I say about my future? Unless I find work, I will have to leave school. I can't pay for paper and pencils. And I can't go to school if my brothers and sisters are starving."

As we drive away from the government buildings, clouds of dust rise from the roads and even the men walking on the streets pull scarves over their faces to protect their eyes and mouths. This is the regular Kabul dust-storm that rises up every afternoon. One returning Afghan told me that in his childhood, before the wars, they never used to have this weather, these clouds of dust blocking out the sunlight and surrounding the mountains with what looks like drifting smoke. He was probably right, since this drought started only a few years ago, but his statement sounded metaphorical—as if the very earth had begun to choke on its burden of misery.

The idea that Afghanistan was destroyed by war was only an image to me until I actually saw Kabul, with the rubble and ruins stretching for mile after mile into the bleak mountains, like a film set designer's vision of a city after a nuclear war. I had to keep reminding myself that Kabul was not always a dystopian city—that once, in the 1970s and 1980s, it was cosmopolitan, with women walking down the streets in miniskirts, crowded jazz clubs and colourful parks. It's also important to remember that Afghan women were not always victims. In the 80s, 40% of doctors and 50% of university students in Kabul were women—and though such liberation did not extend throughout Afghanistan, many urban, educated women lived lives of relative freedom.

But one thing that astounded me was that even those women who have lived all their lives in the most traditional sections of society can still speak a language of resistance. One day, for instance, I visited Sarasia, a bleak little village west of Kabul. Women here live close to the edge; even the village well, after three years of drought, is no longer working, so the women and children traipse across the fields to the neighbouring village every day to collect water. In one of the stark white houses, a literacy class is in progress. The women in this class couldn't be further from the educated elite. Soraya, for instance, is a widow of 50 and has been illiterate all her life. "If you are illiterate, it is as if you are blind," she says. Her eldest son doesn't want her to learn to read, but she has finally won his permission because this class is run by women for women in their own village.

In this village, all the women wear burkas; they always have. None can leave the village without the permission of the men in her family, and none of the women in the room has had any formal education. And yet, somehow, they have kept alive the idea of a different society. Aisha, a middle-aged woman whose husband is too old to work, says, "Because we are uneducated, we can't speak out and defend our rights. We don't want that for our daughters. We want them to know how to speak up in front of outsiders." Again and again, I ask if all the women they know, even in the most traditional families, feel the same. They almost get angry trying to convince me, and the hot little room seems to get hotter as they all speak at once. "Of course we want more freedom," says Soraya. "Even women who are not allowed to come to this class want that. But our husbands and brothers and fathers don't want it. The mullahs keep saying freedom is not good for us."

The literacy course in Sarasia is funded by the Revolutionary Association of the Women of Afghanistan [RAWA]. This extraordinary organisation has been going since 1977 and is a testament to the determined resilience of Afghan women. The thousands of RAWA members have worked underground and in exile for nearly 30 years—against the Soviet regime, the mujaheddin, the Taliban—and they are now stronger than ever. But although RAWA is beginning to operate more openly, most of its work is still anonymous and underground. Oddly, despite the west's much-touted support for a more liberal society, RAWA has never received support from any government.

RAWA's Efforts to Educate Women

But RAWA's members are still agitating for women's equality and a secular government, and they are also passionately involved in rebuilding civil society. In contrast to some of the rather chaotic government and non-governmental projects, the couple of RAWA schemes I see, in Sarasia and Kabul, are models of good organisation and sustainability. One day, I visit one of their schools in Kabul, which operates in the family home of a former radio broadcaster from Mazar-i-Sharif, who prefers to remain anonymous.

On the street outside, it is the usual Kabul scene: heaps of rubbish, a blinding glare, dust-filled air. Then you push open a large blue door to a courtyard. Here, somebody is growing herbs and vegetables, and two white-and-yellow butterflies dip their wings over the thick green fronds of radish plants. Under awnings on the sides of the courtyard, one group of women is spelling out its Persian lesson and another is cutting bright cloth, learning to make shirts.

One of the teachers here is Zahmina Nyamati. She is 42, with a weather-beaten, sensible face. [In the early 1980's], Zahmina was like Zohal Faiz Mohammed, an optimistic science graduate from Kabul University. She married a civil servant and had five children. But after her husband died [in 1995], she took her family to live in a refugee camp in Pakistan. She became a servant for Pakistani families all day and sewed all night, trying to earn enough money to keep her children in school. As she speaks, the tears run down her face. She doesn't try to wipe them away.

"I have good memories in my life, from my childhood, and when I was first married. But then everything was lost. I worked in houses where I was dirt, and I was allowed as a great favour to collect the food they were going to throw out to take to my children.

"When I got married, I thought at least we will live in peace. At least we will have a simple house, where we can say, 'It's my room'; at least when my children go to school, they can say, 'These are my shoes, this is my pencil.' But my children sit alone. They never play with other children. When I come home, they say, 'What have you brought us?' And I can't say anything. My life is over. But I want a better life for them. This is why I work all day and all night. I must be strong. I pray every day, 'God make me strong.'"

After her class is over, Zahmina takes me to her home. This neighbourhood is what most of Kabul looks like—a slum, where the sewers drain into the street, and the street is just packed dust. She lives in one room with her four children, one of whom is handicapped and lies on the floor, unable to walk or crawl. There is no furniture except for one bed heaped with scraps of clothes and blankets. After the Taliban fell, like hundreds of thousands of others, Zahmina returned to Kabul with the help of the UN refugee agency, which gives returning refugees $10–$30 per person. Zahmina's family also received two plastic sheets, two blankets and three bags of flour. First, they went to live in Chehl Sutoon, a ruined area where there is no running water, no roofs, no windows. Now they feel lucky to have found one room with a roof. If it wasn't for RAWA, she might soon be begging like the other women whose claw-like hands grab at you on the streets.

Looking to the Future

As we talk about the past, she asks her daughter, a flesh-faced girl of 12, to get out the photographs. Alya pulls the box from under the bed. The few family snaps show a big, happy family at birthday parties, sitting around with the children on their parents' laps, a cake and watermelon and biscuits on a table, balloons in children's hands. Alya and her brothers handle the pictures reverently, dreaming over them.

I ask Zahmina if she has any hopes for the future. She doesn't hesitate. "I hope, it is my only wish, that the international organisations that have promised to help Afghanistan will fulfil their promises, especially for women. And I have heard our politicians talk about women's rights. I hope Afghan women will achieve these. We have known such suffering for these 23 years. We just want to give our children what they need, so they can grow up to fulfil their dreams." I am struck once again, struck with an almost physical shock, by the way in which Afghan women are facing the future with such stony determination.

Alya listens to us talk. The little girl, who has grown up in a refugee camp, then moved to a ruin and then to a slum, is slender and bright-eyed in green shalwar kameez. I ask what she thinks she will do in the future. "I will be a doctor!" she says determinedly.

Afghanistan Remains Oppressed by Fundamentalists

By the Revolutionary Association of the Women of Afghanistan

The Revolutionary Association of the Women of Afghanistan, or RAWA, is an organization based in Afghanistan that fights for political and social justice for the people of Afghanistan. The following statement was issued by RAWA on the first anniversary of the September 11, 2001, attacks on the World Trade Center and the Pentagon. In it, RAWA argues that the situation in Afghanistan has not improved since the Taliban was deposed. That the regime has, in fact, been replaced by similar fundamentalists who continue to threaten the basic human rights of the Afghan people. In RAWA's view, the only way to ensure social justice and bring peace and stability to Afghanistan is to completely eradicate fundamentalist leadership and to replace it with a secular democracy.

R AWA [the Revolutionary Association of the Women of Afghanistan] joins with the rest of the civilized world in remembering the innocent lives lost on September 11th, as well as all those others lost to terrorism and oppression throughout the world. It is with great sadness that RAWA sees other people experiencing the pain that the women, children and men of Afghanistan have long suffered at the hands of fundamentalist terrorists.

For ten long years the people of Afghanistan—Afghan women in particular—have been crushed and brutalized, first under the chains and atrocities of the "Northern Alliance" fundamentalists, then under those of the Taliban. During all this period, the governments of the Western powers were bent on finding ways to "work with" these criminals. These Western governments did not lose much sleep over the

Revolutionary Association of the Women of Afghanistan, "Fundamentalism Is the Enemy of All Civilized Humanity," http://rawa.fancymarketing.net, September 11, 2002. Copyright © 2002 by the Revolutionary Association of the Women of Afghanistan. Reproduced by permission.

daily grind of abject misery our people were enduring under the domination of these terrorist bands. To them it did not matter so very much that human rights and democratic principles were being trampled on a daily basis in an inconceivable manner. What was important was to "work with" the religio-fascists to have Central Asian oil pipelines extended to accessible ports of shipment.

Immediately after the September 11 tragedy the US military might moved into action to punish its erstwhile hirelings. A captive, bleeding, devastated, hungry, pauperized, drought-stricken and ill-starred Afghanistan was bombed into oblivion by the most advanced and sophisticated weaponry ever created in human history. Innocent lives, many more than those who lost their lives in the September 11 atrocity, were taken. Even joyous wedding gatherings were not spared. The Taliban regime and its al-Qaeda support were toppled without any significant dent in their human combat resources. What was not done away with was the sinister shadow of terrorist threat over the whole world and its alter ego, fundamentalist terrorism.

Neither opium cultivation nor warlordism have been eradicated in Afghanistan. There is neither peace nor stability in this tormented country, nor has there been any relief from the scourges of extreme pauperization, prostitution, and wanton plunder. Women feel much more insecure than in the past. The bitter fact that even the personal security of the President of the country cannot be maintained without recourse to foreign bodyguards and the recent terrorist acts in our country speak eloquent volumes about the chaotic and terrorist-ridden situation of the country. Why is it so? Why has the thunderous uproar in the aftermath of September 11 resulted in nothing? For the following reasons which RAWA has reiterated time and again:

1. For the people of Afghanistan, it is "out of the frying pan, into the fire". Instead of the Taliban terrorists, Jihadi terrorists of the "Northern Alliance" have been installed in power. The Jihadi and the Taliban fundamentalists share a common ideology; their differences are the usual differences between brethren-in-creed.

2. For the past more or less twenty years, Osama bin Laden has had Afghan fundamentalists on his payroll and has been paying their leaders considerable stipends. He and [Taliban leader] Mullah Omar, together with a band of followers equipped with the necessary communication resources, can live for many years under the protection of different fundamentalist bands in Afghanistan and Pakistan and continue to plot against the people of Afghanistan and the rest of humankind.

3. The Taliban and the al-Qaeda phenomena, as manifestations of an ideology and a political culture infesting an Islamic country,

could only have been uprooted by a popular insurrection and the strengthening and coming to power of secular democratic forces. Such a purge cannot be effected solely with the physical elimination of the likes of Osama and Mullah Omar.

The "Northern Alliance" can never sincerely want the total elimination of the Taliban and the al-Qaeda, as such elimination would mean the end of the *raison d'être* of the backing and support extended to them by foreign forces presently dominant in the country. This was the rationale behind RAWA's slogan for the overthrow of the Taliban and al-Qaeda through popular insurrection. Unfortunately, before such popular insurrection could come about, the Taliban and al-Qaeda forfeited their positions to the "brethren of the 'Northern Alliance'" without suffering any crippling decimation.

With their second occupation of Kabul, the "Northern Alliance" thwarted any hopes for a radical, meaningful change. They are themselves now the source and root of insecurity, the disgraceful police atmosphere of the Loya Jirga [grand assembly, held in June 2002], rampant terrorism, gagging of democracy, atrocious violations of human rights, mourning pauperization, prostitution and corruption, the flourishing of poppy cultivation, failure of beginning to reconstruct, and a host of further unlisted evils, too many to enumerate.

Oppression and crimes against women are rife in different forms throughout the country. RAWA has always maintained that the fundamentalists' rabid hatred of women as equal human beings—be they fundamentalists of the Jihadi brand or of the Taliban one—is not due merely to their unhealthy upbringing or morbid mind frame, but emanates from their religio-fascistic ideological world outlook. As long as such an ideology exists, propped up by military forces available at its disposal, neither crazed misogyny nor a myriad of shameful social evils associated with it can be eradicated. This is not a problem that can be dealt with by the creation of a "Ministry of Women's Affairs" nor by the presence of a couple of token women in high government positions. To hope for the attainment of freedom, democracy and equality within the framework of a corrupt, religion-based, ethnochauvinistic system is either self-delusion or hypocrisy—or both.

We find no happiness in the fact that RAWA's predictions in regard to the consequences of the re-domination of the "Northern Alliance" have once again been borne out. Those who claimed that the "Northern Alliance" were better than, and therefore preferable to, the Taliban must wake up and apologise to our people for their noxious sermons. The establishment of democracy and social justice can be possible only with the overthrow of fundamentalist domination as a prime precondition. This cannot be achieved without an organised and irreconcilable campaign of the women masses against fundamentalism, its agents and apologists.

Some politically bankrupt entities who have no shame in grovelling to the "Northern Alliance" in the hope of securing positions and feathering their nests, label RAWA as "Maoist" [after Chinese Communist Party leader chairman Mao] and "radical" because of our decisive and irreconcilable stances and viewpoints. But does the current situation in the country prove the fallacy of RAWA's positions or do they give a slap in the face to the ladies and gentleman with the penchant for being colluding and mealy-mouthed? The assassinations of a vice president and a cabinet minister and the ban on investigating these murders, the discovery of mass graves, the banning of women singers and artists and showing of dancing on TV, the censorship of the media, arbitrary *fatwas* [religious rulings or edicts] of *kofr* [heresy] and apostasy against women, gang rapes of even expatriate women working for international NGOs, the disgusting campaign of making an idol out of [deceased Northern Alliance general] Ahmad Shah Masoud, are these not enough to bring home the realisation that indulgence and permissiveness towards rabid dogs only serve to make them more ferocious?

RAWA's experience in fighting fundamentalism, particularly during the past 10 years, motivates us to be all the more persistent in our attempts to mobilise women even in the most remote corners of our country. At the same time, we shall not desist from pursuing an irreconcilable policy towards fundamentalism and standing in solidarity with all pro-democracy forces. We staunchly believe that in addition to causing the tragic deaths of over 3,000 innocent Americans and non-Americans and the sorrow and bereavement of tens of thousands more, the monstrous terrorist attack of September 11 showed the world what a nefarious pestilence fundamentalism is; it showed the world the sort of inferno the peoples of Afghanistan, Iran, Algeria, Sudan and other such countries live in.

Fundamentalism is the mortal enemy of civilised humanity; to address it demands the consolidated action of all freedom-loving nations of the world. The present "world anti-terrorism coalition" has been debased by innumerable ambiguities and impurities of purpose, motivation and objectives. The contradictions between world powers will spell its doom. Therefore, it behoves anti-fundamentalist individuals and organisations working for social justice the world over to draw together without hesitation to contain and ultimately stamp out, once and for all, the vermin of fundamentalism, so that the tragedy of September 11 will never be repeated, neither in America nor anywhere else.

RAWA takes pride in the fact that up till now we have been able to establish contact with a considerable number of anti-terrorist organisations on all five continents and enjoy their moral and material support. However, for the purpose of waging a swifter and more encompassing fight against terrorism, it is necessary for such solidarity to be expanded and strengthened. In this connection we shake the hands of all freedom-loving individuals and organisations.

We would like to avail ourselves of this opportunity to once again extend our heartfelt condolences to all those who lost their loved one in the savage calamity of September 11, as well as to the friends and families of those innocent compatriots—for all we know, anti-Taliban and anti-"Northern Alliance"—who were blown to shreds by American aerial bombardment. We sincerely hope that a vast number of those who are bereaved and grieving for their loved ones will, sooner or later, join the ranks of the legions mobilising against fundamentalist fascism in their respective countries and on an international level.

No to Al-Qaeda, No to the Taliban, No to the "Northern Alliance"! Long Live a Free, Democratic and Blossoming Afghanistan! Victory in the Decisive War to the Very End of Afghan Women Against Fundamentalism and for Democracy! Long Live International Solidarity Against Fundamentalist Terrorism!

CHAPTER 3

Afghanistan and Its Neighbors: Security in Central Asia

A Stable Afghanistan Is Crucial to the Peace of Central Asia

By Ahmed Rashid

Ahmed Rashid is the Pakistan, Afghanistan, and Central Asia correspondent for the Far Eastern Economic Review *and the* Daily Telegraph. *In the following selection, Rashid examines the importance of stability in Afghanistan for the continued security of Central Asia as a whole. The author argues that Afghanistan's long, destabilizing war, its propensity for attracting and harboring militant Islamic fundamentalists, and its difficult and complex relationship with its close neighbor, Pakistan, are all factors that contribute to the instability of the entire region as well as Afghanistan itself.*

C entral Asia's Muslim neighbors to the south represent a plethora of competing interests and rivalries, which the Central Asian leaders have been trying to juggle for a decade. Even as these neighbors—Pakistan, Iran, and Turkey—rhetorically pledge cooperation with Central Asia in such multilateral organizations as the Economic Cooperation Organization, the Organization of the Islamic Conference, and the United Nations, their inherent rivalries and individual agendas have proved to be destabilizing factors. Farther afield, parties and individuals in the Arab Gulf states have provided funds and backing to the IMU [Islamic Movement of Uzbekistan], whilst the wider Muslim world has made only marginal efforts to bring Central Asia into the world community.

The most pressing issues for Central Asia are the continuing civil

Ahmed Rashid, *Jihad: The Rise of Militant Islam in Central Asia.* New York: Penguin Books, 2002.
Copyright © 2002 by Yale University. Reproduced by permission.

war in Afghanistan and the Taliban's role in giving sanctuary to the IMU and other militant Islamic groups. The tragedy is that like Russia and the United States, Central Asia's Muslim neighbors have fed this civil war, arming and funding one side or the other and drawing in the republics regardless of their own desires.

The Threat from Afghanistan

The crisis in Afghanistan is the single most important external factor in the growing instability in Central Asia. Afghanistan has long been linked to Central Asia, historically and culturally. Over the centuries the two regions have been joined in various empires, and ethnic groups in northern Afghanistan come from the same stock as Central Asian Uzbeks, Tajiks, and Turkmen. The ethnic, social, cultural, and political ties between Afghanistan and Central Asia are thus deeply rooted, and the give and take between the two regions today cannot be seen as an aberration of history but rather as a continuation of the historical process that was briefly interrupted by the seventy-four years of the Soviet Union.

In a historical sense, when the IMU retreats to Taliban-controlled Afghanistan, it is only continuing an ancient tradition of demanding and receiving hospitality and sanctuary. In the twentieth century, guests in Afghanistan have included the rulers of Bukhara, Khiva, and Kokand after the Russian Revolution; Basmachis who were escaping the Bolsheviks; and members of the Tajikistan IRP [Islamic Renaissance Party] who took refuge during Tajikistan's civil war. And like the IMU, both the Basmachis and the IRP continued fighting their Central Asian wars from bases in Afghanistan. For their part Afghans have also taken refuge in Central Asia, particularly since the fighting began in 1979.

But neither tradition nor the proverbial Muslim hospitality can account completely for the Taliban's willingness to give sanctuary to the IMU. Before the events of September 11, 2001, the Taliban played host to most of the extremist Islamic groups in the Muslim world, and their motives have clearly been militant. In Afghanistan these groups fight for the Taliban, and in return they receive military training, battle experience, weapons, funding, access to the drug trade, and contacts with the whole world of Islamic radicalism.

Centuries of history also do not explain why Afghanistan should become the host for the world's Islamic extremists. That answer lies in more current events; in the efforts during the 1980s by the United States to foment rebellion against the Soviet Union. When the CIA funneled arms to the Afghan Mujahedeen via Pakistan's Interservices Intelligence (ISI), the ISI gave preference to the radical Afghan Islamic parties—which could more easily be turned into an engine of anti-Soviet jihad—and pushed aside moderate Afghan nationalist and Islamic parties. At that time the CIA made no objections to this policy. The Taliban are the heirs of that war and that favoritism, although their harsh interpretation of Deobandi Islam and their desire to transform Afghanistan to fit their interpretation of sharia [the Islamic legal system and code based on the Koran] are foreign to Afghan's Islamic traditions.

Taliban Ideology Imported from Pakistan

The Taliban reflect none of the major Islamicist trends that were earlier prevalent in Afghanistan or that emerged during the jihad of the 1980s. They are not inspired by the Ikhwan-ul-Muslimeen (Muslim Brotherhood)—the earliest Islamic radicals in the twentieth century—they do not follow the path of the mystical Sufis. They do not base their Islam on the ulema [the body of scholars on Islamic theology]. All these strands of Islam either have historical roots in Afghanistan or arose during the jihad. Nor do the Taliban have a secure tribal base or tribal legitimacy amongst their own majority ethnic group, the Pashtuns, the largest ethnic group in Afghanistan. Many of the Pashtun tribal elite refuse to recognize the Taliban and have fled to Pakistan. In fact, they fit nowhere in the Islamic or nationalist spectrum of ideas and movements that emerged in Afghanistan between 1979 and 1994. Instead, their ideology of Deobandi Islam is largely imported from Pakistan. Their initial popularity in 1994–96 was due not merely to their Islamic zeal but to other factors operating in Afghanistan—the revival of Pashtun nationalism in the face of Tajik control of Kabul and the need to restore law and order, reopen the roads, and end rapacious warlordism—that the Taliban made part of their early agenda, before they began to host foreign militant groups in 1996.

But the Taliban had no international Islamic agenda until they met up with Osama bin Laden and other non-Afghan Islamic groups after they captured Kabul in 1996. A few Taliban leaders had earlier dreamed of "liberating" the holy Muslim cities of Bukhara and Samarkand [both in Uzbekistan], but most had no idea where Bukhara and Samarkand even were. The tens of thousands of Pakistani militants, and the thousands of Central Asians, Arabs, Africans, and East Asians who have fought for the Taliban since that time, have brought with them a global perspective of Islamic radicalism that the Taliban have adopted as their own. Most recently, bin Laden and his Arab followers have become part of the decision-making process within the Taliban leadership, pushing the Taliban to expand their goals beyond

Afghanistan into Central Asia. I have explored this issue more fully in my recent book on the Taliban; here suffice it to say that the Taliban now depend on these foreign fighters to expand their ideology as much as the foreign groups depend on the Taliban for sanctuary.

Until Afghanistan is at peace—or at least until the present Taliban leaders are removed from power, most likely as a result of the U.S.-led military campaign aimed at Osama bin Laden—it is highly unlikely that the Taliban will change their policies.[1] Lacking any desire to build a modern political state, the Taliban see the continuation of the present war against the anti-Taliban United Front [also known as the Northern Alliance] as the only means of securing the loyalty of their fighters. Thus even if the United Front were defeated and forced to retreat into Tajikistan, the present Taliban leaders would probably become even more aggressive against the Central Asian regimes. Conjuring up new enemies is the best way to fuel the permanent state of jihad, the only thing that keeps the army united and motivated. The first enemy to be singled out would probably be Tajikistan because of the Russian forces based there; later would come Uzbekistan. The Taliban's tragedy is that their leaders fear that peace will destroy the movement because they have no agenda for the reconstruction of the country. Thus they are unwilling to change their policies.

Although the start of the U.S. bombing campaign against the Taliban on October 7 [2001] . . . made it virtually certain that the Taliban leadership will be eliminated from Afghanistan, once the war is over there will be an intense tussle between the ethnic groups, warlords, and remaining Taliban defectors as to who will form the new government. Afghanistan's best bet is for Afghans to rally around the former king Zahir Shah, who has set out to build a broad-based, multiethnic coalition to oppose the Taliban. This coalition could be the basis of a new, internationally accepted government in Kabul. However, such efforts will be successful only if the West remains in Afghanistan after the shooting stops. Not only will U.N. peace-keeping forces need to stay for a while to stabilize the region, but massive funds must be available for the reconstruction of the country. The reconstruction of the region will require a determined and prolonged international effort to help Afghanistan back into the global community.

Pakistan: Educating Islam's Militants

Pakistan did not create the Taliban, but the Taliban could not have survived amongst Afghanistan's warring factions without the support of Islamabad. Indeed, fear of Pakistan's influence in the region has been

1. The entire Taliban leadership was driven from power in 2001 by a U.S.-led coalition.

a critical factor in the mobilization of the Central Asian states (with the exception of Turkmenistan) against the Taliban. Central Asian leaders also believe (correctly) that the ISI has until recently been supporting the IMU and other radical Islamic groups in their countries. These men do not forget that in the 1980s, when they held power under the Soviet Union, the military regime of Pakistan's President Muhammad Zia ul Haq encouraged the Afghan Mujahedeen to attack Central Asia and that the CIA supplied arms to the Mujahedeen for this purpose through the ISI. In fact, the aversion of these leaders to even the most peaceful Islamic practice or piety arose in part as a result of the Afghan war, when Pakistan was on the other side. Pakistan's subsequent support for the Taliban and the Pashtuns, and President Pervez Musharraf's rejection in the summer of 2001 of non-Pashtun ethnic groups in Afghanistan as irrelevant to Pakistan's interests, has further antagonized the leaders of Central Asia [by overwhelmingly favoring Pashtun interests]. Musharraf's myopic foreign policy since he seized power in a military coup in 1999 did much to further alienate Pakistan's northern neighbors.

Although successive Pakistani governments have repeatedly promised the Central Asian leaders that they would curb the support given by the ISI to Pakistan's Islamic parties, the Taliban, and other militant groups in Central Asia, and forbid Central Asian militants to study in Pakistani madrassahs, Islamabad has failed to implement these measures out of self-interest and the fear of an Islamic backlash within Pakistan. In fact, in recent years Central Asian and Uijhur [Muslims of the formerly independent Republic of East Turkistan now part of China] militants have been pouring into the country to study in the huge network of Deobandi madrassahs. The IMU, the HT [or Hizb ut-Fahir al-Islam; a fundamentalist, nonviolent Islamic movement], and the Chechen rebels have sent many of their young men to study in Pakistan, whilst Pakistani Islamic parties continue to show off their Central Asian students as proof of their influence in the region. Even more than the battlefields of Afghanistan, this madrassah education and the culture of jihad it inspires is turning out ideologically committed Islamic radicals for future fighting in Central Asia.

Pakistan's policies have been driven in part by the mutual animosity between India and Pakistan and Islamabad's fears of Indian hegemony in South Asia. India's earlier influence in Kabul has significantly affected Pakistan's relationship with Afghanistan, which is why Pakistan has wanted to see a friendly Pashtun government there since the 1950s. And since the 1980s Pakistan has seen Afghanistan as a source of what President Zia ul Haq called "strategic depth" in the event of war with India. Determined to deny India any influence in Afghanistan, Pakistan in 1989 helped fuel what was originally an indigenous popular uprising in Indian Kashmir. When India and the United States accused Pakistan of training and arming Kashmiri and Pakistani militants on its soil to fight in Kashmir—thereby sponsoring terrorism—the Taliban provided a convenient deniability factor. Just as when the Taliban send Pakistani or Chinese militants to join the IMU so they can deny that they support them, so Pakistan has sent many of its Kashmiri fighters to train in Afghanistan with the Taliban. Several Pakistani groups [made] it a matter of policy to let their young guerrillas fight first for the Taliban before they are moved to the more arduous guerrilla fronts in Kashmir.

After the 1991 collapse of the Soviet Union, Zia ul Haq's references to the need for strategic depth in Central Asia as well as Afghanistan took on a greater significance. For a time it appeared to some Pakistanis that the Islamic revival in Central Asia and the civil war in Tajikistan would blow away the present generation of Soviet-trained Central Asian leaders. Thus Pakistan's military stepped up its efforts to create a client Pashtun government in Kabul, in the hope that such a government would give Pakistan easy, exclusive access to Central Asia. Moderates who argued in 1991 that Islamabad should instead support a quick end to the Afghan civil war in the hope that whichever government came to power in Kabul would provide trade routes to Pakistan were quickly silenced. The military extended the idea of strategic depth to Central Asia as a natural corollary to their policies in Afghanistan, even as Pakistan's civilian governments tried to follow more positive policies and build economic ties with Central Asia.

In 1991 the elected government of Prime Minister Nawaz Sharif sought a new relationship with Central Asia built on trade, pipeline routes, investment, and joint economic development. This made eminent good sense. Karachi [Pakistan] is the nearest port city for the Central Asian states, and Islamabad is closer to Tashkent than it is to Karachi. The distance from Dushanbe [capital of Tajikistan] to Karachi by road is only 1,700 miles compared to 2,125 miles to the Iranian port of Bandar Abbas, 2,625 miles to Rostov-on-Don in western Russia, and 5,940 miles to Vladivostok in eastern Russia. All that was needed to realize these opportunities was peace in Afghanistan. But the ISI consistently blocked this outcome. The attempts by Sharif and his minister for economic affairs Sardar Asif Ali were also undercut by the arrival in Central Asia of Pakistani Islamic parties, who viewed the region as virgin territory, ripe for recruitment to their particular brand of Islam. Qazi Hussein Ahmad, the chief of the powerful Jamiat-i-Islami party, urged Sharif "to provide Central Asia with Islamic guidance rather than economic aid." At the same time several Pakistani and Arab groups sympathetic to Wahhabism were being funded by Saudi Arabia to make inroads into Central Asia. The Pakistani extremist groups Lashkar-i-Jhangvi and Sipah-i-Sahaba, initially funded by Saudi Arabia, have militants fighting with the IMU.

By 1994, when the Taliban emerged, Pakistan's hopes of forging new productive links with Central Asia had virtually collapsed, apart from a blossoming relationship with neutral Turkmenistan. Ironically, it was not the ISI but Prime Minister Benazir Bhutto, the most liberal, secular leader in Pakistan's recent history, who delivered the coup de grâce to a new relationship with Central Asia. Rather than support a wider peace process in Afghanistan that would have opened up the natural north-south trade routes between Central Asia and Pakistan through Afghanistan, Bhutto backed the Taliban, in a rash and presumptuous policy to create a new western-orientated trade and pipeline route from Turkmenistan through southern Afghanistan to Pakistan, for which the Taliban would provide security. The ISI soon supported this policy because its Afghan protégé Gulbuddin Hekmatyar had made no headway in capturing Kabul, and the Taliban appeared to be strong enough to do so. The idea that Pakistan would ignore the rest of Central Asia in favor of Turkmenistan whilst backing the Taliban in Afghanistan created even greater suspicion amongst Central Asia's leaders about Pakistan's intentions.

In turn Pakistan became more anxious as the Central Asian leaders gravitated back towards Islamabad's two long-standing enemies, Russia and India, whilst rivals Iran and Turkey began to make inroads into the region. The military, which has always been the key formulator of Pakistan's foreign policy, saw little hope of persuading the Central Asian leaders to change their strategic intentions and befriend Islamabad. As Pakistan became more wedded to the Taliban, more hostile to the anti-Taliban alliance, and more embroiled in the conflict in Kashmir—which escalated dramatically in 1999 because of Pakistan's military incursion in Kargil—Islamabad's antagonism to the Central Asian leaders increased. These feelings were reciprocated by the Central Asian leaders, who blamed every significant northward advance of the Taliban on Pakistani military support or collusion.

It is widely believed that the ISI's discreet support of the IMU, which included giving refuge to Yuldeshev [founder and military leader of the IMU] in the 1990s and allowing [Juma] Namangani's frequent clandestine visits to Pakistan, has remained fairly consistent. The ISI sees the IMU as a force that may not be strong enough to seize power in Uzbekistan but that can nonetheless be a catalyst in the shake-up of Central Asia's leadership. Yet Pakistan's military regime is hedging its bets; it also predicts that it can win back the friendship of Central Asia by acting as a mediator between the regimes and the IMU. Thus Pakistan does not necessarily intend to support the ideological Islamic views of the IMU or help bring it to power but rather intends to use the IMU as leverage within Central Asia. At the same time senior ISI officers are convinced that the IMU has close intelligence links to Russia that would explain the group's freedom of action on the Afghanistan-Tajikistan border. These ties make the IMU an unreliable long-term partner, compared to, say, the anti-Russian Taliban. The ISI does not trust the IMU, believing that Pakistan is locked in a covert power struggle with Russia for influence over it but at the same time it wishes to keep the IMU on its payroll for tactical reasons.

Despite Pakistan's persistent denials that it supports the IMU, until September 11 the military regime appeared set on a course where it followed a state policy of friendly relations with the Central Asian governments but at the same time backed dissident groups such as the IMU in order to win more leverage over these regimes. Islamabad believes that the present generation of Central Asian leaders must be replaced by more Islamic-orientated leaders who would look to Pakistan, rather than India and Russia, for support. Thus a vicious cycle of suspicion, accusation, and counteraccusation now mars Pakistan's relationship with the Central Asian regimes.

At the same time Pakistan's frequent internal crises have weakened state power, increasing the influence of nonstate actors. These include extremist Islamic parties, with their madrassah culture and jihadi strategy; Arab terrorist groups such as Al Qaeda; the truck and transport smuggling mafias; and drug traffickers—all of whom have close links to the Taliban and the IMU quite independent of the ISI and its policies. The result has been an explosion of self-interest groups in Pakistan, both Islamic and non-Islamic, who have benefited from the Afghan civil war and Islamic insurgency in Central Asia. These groups see no need for peace. The weakening of state authority, not just in Pakistan but across the entire region, would enable their business interests and Islamic agendas to flourish.

But the events of September 11 have forced the military regime of President Musharraf to make a dramatic U turn. U.S. president George W. Bush's ultimatum—that states must be either with the United States or against it—left Pakistan with little choice but to cease its support for the Taliban and help the U.S. effort to defeat both it and Al Qaeda. Musharraf's move has proved deeply controversial inside Pakistan as the militant Islamic parties oppose his decision to side with the Western alliance and have staged protests in the streets of Pakistan. The majority of Pakistan's population, however, has supported the decision. Pakistan now has a chance to change its policies towards the entire region and set its own house in order.

If Pakistan goes along with the elimination of the Taliban and the IMU, and supports a new, internationally accepted government in Kabul, it can win back the trust of the Central Asian states. The move would give Pakistan renewed opportunities to be involved in new oil and gas pipelines from Central Asia that would cross Afghanistan and Pakistan to the Gulf. Eventually, the military regime's policy reversal on Afghanistan will also necessitate a reconsideration of Pakistan's support for the Kashmiri separatists, forcing the country to build better relations with India. Lastly, the regime will need to clamp down on the madrassah culture that has spawned so much unrest in the region. This moment of opportunity for Pakistan—a chance to reestablish its international credibility, end its diplomatic isolation in the region, and become a partner rather than a rival of Central Asia—will require that the military and the ISI relinquish their strategic vision of the past fifty years and adopt a strategy which makes friends rather than enemies in Central Asia.

The War in Afghanistan Has Resulted in an Increased U.S. Military Presence in Central Asia

By J. Eric Duskin

As the military offensive in Afghanistan began to turn to the daunting task of peacekeeping, the Bush administration sought to widen the scope of America's involvement in the nations adjacent to Afghanistan. As reported by J. Eric Duskin, an assistant professor of history at Christopher Newport University and a Fulbright Scholar now living in Central Asia, the war in Afghanistan gave the United States an added incentive to ensure stability in the region. Duskin explores the goals of further U.S. involvement in Central Asian affairs, such as securing Central Asia's rich oil supply, maintaining stability in the region, and introducing political and economic reform in the area. The increased U.S. presence in Central Asia may, in the author's opinion, ultimately have little to do with Afghanistan directly and may create a perception that America is excessively interfering with Central Asian affairs, which in turn could undermine the stability it seeks to create.

A giant statue of Lenin [the founder of the Russian Communist Party] still towers over the central square in Bishkek, capital of

J. Eric Duskin, "Permanent Installation," *In These Times*, vol. 26, April 29, 2002, pp. 19–21. Copyright © 2002 by *In These Times*. Reproduced by permission.

the former Soviet Kyrgyz Republic. Where once the statue's raised right arm pointed to a glorious socialist future, today Lenin seems to be directing attention to the American soldiers on the city's outskirts. But everyone in this quiet little city of tree-lined streets and Stalin-era apartment buildings is already talking about the Americans. No one here can quite believe that thousands of U.S. troops and hundreds of NATO planes will soon be based nearby.

At Bishkek's Manas Airport, Marat could only shake his head as he watched an Air Force C-130 cargo plane thunder down the runway. A university student and Bishkek resident with Russian and Ukrainian parents, Marat was shocked to see American soldiers occupying the main terminal's top floor and neighboring buildings. Across the street from the terminal, hundreds of GIs were diligently constructing a vast new complex of buildings and sheds. As he peered through a fence, Marat said that until now he had considered talk of American imperialism just to be Communist propaganda. Yet the next day, Marat and his friends went to U.S. military headquarters at the Hyatt Regency and applied for jobs.

Before the war in Afghanistan, few Americans had ever heard of Kyrgyzstan—or the other new Central Asian states of Kazakhstan, Tajikistan, Uzbekistan and Turkmenistan, which all now figure prominently in America's foreign policy plans. The State Department and Pentagon have quietly cobbled together a bold strategy for American military expansion into this region, building military facilities in Kyrgyzstan, Uzbekistan and Tajikistan and staking claim to a land of deserts, vast steppe and towering mountain ranges along the ancient Silk Road, where no Western country has ever stationed troops before.

The five Central Asian countries, which comprise an area about half the size of the continental United States, have been part of a Russian sphere of influence since the 19th century. Most Russians still consider these countries on Russia's southern border, and the millions of ethnic Russians who live there, as essential to Russian interests. China also views the prospect of permanent American air bases with alarm. What's more, not only is the region rife with religious and ethnic tensions, but all five countries have authoritarian governments responsible for well-documented human rights abuses. Yet neither the billions of dollars that may be spent here nor the risks of antagonizing the neighboring nuclear powers have attracted much critical attention from the U.S. media.

The Groundwork for a Long Stay

American military forces first increased their presence in the region to prepare for the bombing of Afghanistan. In September [2001], the

Bush administration asked Uzbek President Islam Karimov for permission to operate out of the old Soviet Khanabad air base near the Afghan border. By October, the United States and Uzbekistan had announced an accord granting American use of multiple Uzbek air fields in return for promises to protect Uzbek security. Two months later, the Tajik government officially announced that it would provide air bases for U.S. forces. And in mid-December, the United States and Kyrgyzstan signed the agreement to build a 37-acre base in Bishkek that will eventually house 3,000 troops and an unspecified number of NATO aircraft.

A parade of U.S. officials—including Secretary of State Colin Powell, Defense Secretary Donald Rumsfeld, Senate Majority Leader Tom Daschle and Gen. Tommy Franks—has visited the Central Asian countries in recent months to confer with the local leaders. Although Franks stated in a recent visit to Bishkek that "we have no plans to build a permanent military base" in Central Asia, other evidence indicates that the U.S. plans to remain in the region long after the end of the current fighting in Afghanistan.

While the lease for the air base in Kyrgyzstan is valid for only a year, the extensive construction program at the site indicates that the Americans do not plan to leave anytime soon. Kyrgyz President Askar Akayev has already announced his willingness to renew the lease for as long as necessary. Russian journalists have reported that the United States and Uzbekistan signed an agreement leasing the Khanabad base for 25 years. The Pentagon has denied this report but refused to specify the nature of its agreement with Uzbekistan.

Deputy Defense Secretary Paul Wolfowitz has said that building air bases and conducting joint training exercises with local troops will "send a message to everybody, including important countries like Uzbekistan that . . . we're not just going to forget about them." This sentiment has been echoed by Colin Powell, who told the House International Relations Committee in early February [2002] that "America will have a continuing interest and presence in Central Asia of a kind that we could not have dreamed of before."

Why the Buildup?

Central Asia's strategic importance seems obvious when looking at a map—but a closer analysis raises a number of troubling issues. The new bases would place American forces on China's western frontier where, in combination with bases to China's east and south, they allow the U.S. military to surround the country. These same bases also place American forces on Russia's southern border for the first time. But presumably missiles already target all important sites in Russia and China, so encirclement of these two nuclear powers does nothing to enhance global security.

Bases in the region also would appear to be useful for continuing American operations in Afghanistan—or even in neighboring Iran, which Bush recently singled out as part of the "axis of evil." Yet with aircraft carriers, long-range bombers, and inflight refueling, these new bases would actually do little to extend the reach of American air power. None of the bombers in the recent Afghan campaign came from Central Asian bases.

Neither can the bases be justified by a need for large numbers of ground forces, since no one in Washington is seriously contemplating such a deployment. Nor would these bases do much to help get humanitarian aid to those in need: That task falls mainly to the United Nations and non-governmental organizations such as the Red Cross, which are not normally granted use of American bases.

Furthermore, most experts agree that the possibility of radical Muslims seizing power in the region is remote at best. All five countries have governments with secular orientations, and the vast majority of the Muslims in the region are also largely secular. Most men and women wear Western-style clothing, and alcohol and pork, forbidden under Islamic law, are popular here. Only Tajikistan has a substantial number of fundamentalist Muslims, but Russian troops have been keeping order in that country since a civil war in the early '90s.

If these new U.S. bases aren't necessary for American military requirements, why is the Bush Administration pressing so hard to build them? One high-ranking U.S. diplomat in the region, who spoke off the record, told *In These Times* that "we now have an opportunity to move these countries away from Russia."

The Oil Issue

Many observers also suspect that an important motivation for U.S. expansion into the region is oil. Both Turkmenistan and Kazakhstan have substantial energy reserves. Kazakhstan has led the way in development of its energy sector by encouraging foreign investment; already, several Western oil companies are pumping oil from Kazakh fields in and around the Caspian Sea. [In] October [2001], Kazakhstan opened a pipeline that takes Kazakh oil through Russia to Western markets.

Kazakh President Nursultan Nazarbayev is already exploring options for a second pipeline. Kazakh officials are most seriously considering two possible routes: one that would go through Iran to the Persian Gulf, and another that would go through Azerbaijan and Georgia into Turkey. The United States is trying to influence Nazarbayev's decision and has publicly stated its preference for the pipeline that would send oil to world markets via Turkey, its NATO ally. But Moscow isn't pleased by American prodding for a second Kazakh pipeline. Industry experts predict that Kazakhstan will not have enough oil to justify use of two pipelines for almost a decade, so prompt development of a second pipeline would only reduce the amount of oil piped through Russia, thereby limiting Russian tax income from the oil crossing its border.

So far, Nazarbayev has maintained good relations with both Russia and the United States. He has met frequently in recent months with Russian officials, including President Vladimir Putin and Foreign Minister Ivan Ivanov, and he has been an active participant in the Shanghai Cooperation Organization, a loose coalition of Russia, China, and four of the Central Asian states (excluding Turkmenistan).

Nazarbayev also has met with visiting American officials, and in December [2001] he traveled to the United States to meet with President Bush. While in Washington, the Kazakh foreign minister signed an "Energy Partnership Declaration" with Colin Powell that calls on the United States and Kazakhstan to cooperate in the development of Kazakhstan's energy sector and reaffirms U.S. support for the pipeline to Turkey. The Kazakh media claim that the United States also pledged to support Kazakhstan's bid for membership in the World Trade Organization.

Impact on U.S.-Russia Relations

The ring of new American military bases around Kazakhstan in Kyrgyzstan, Tajikistan and Uzbekistan would help send a message to Kazakh officials that they should consider American preferences when making decisions regarding their oil and gas. But any move away from Russia may anger Kazakhstan's large ethnic Russian minority, which makes up 35 to 40 percent of the population. Moreover, American officials would be wise to recall that Russia's oil and gas reserves are far larger than Kazakhstan's and Turkmenistan's combined. America's desire to develop new oil sources outside the Middle East will require Russian cooperation.

Thus far, the most surprising aspect of America's newfound commitment to Central Asia has been Russia's lack of objections. Publicly, [Russian president Vladimir] Putin has said that the countries of Central Asia are independent and must make their own decisions. Putin has not, however, surrendered Central Asia to the Americans. The Russians have maintained their own strong military presence, with about 20,000 troops in Tajikistan along the Afghan border as well as both troops and military research facilities in Kazakhstan and Kyrgyzstan.

Yet some Russian generals are already blaming Putin for "losing"

Central Asia. Members of the Duma [Russian parliament] have spoken out against the American military bases, and Moscow newspapers routinely decry American advances into the region. Putin cannot ignore the growing outrage forever. When he does decide to raise the issue, he will likely have the backing of China, which has stated that it does not expect the Americans to remain in the region after hostilities in Afghanistan end.

Opportunities for Reform

American officials are quick to point out that their plans for the region include aid for political and economic reform as well as military cooperation. The need for reform is clear. All five countries have authoritarian regimes, and only Kyrgyzstan has a leader who was not a Communist Party boss in Soviet times. Opposition parties are allowed to exist in Kyrgyzstan and Kazakhstan, but even in these countries, elections are neither free nor fair. In Kyrgyzstan, President Akayev had his most popular rivals kept off the ballot in recent elections. The government of Kazakhstan's President Nazarbayev has also routinely harassed the leaders and supporters of rival parties.

Meanwhile, the leaders of Uzbekistan and Turkmenistan, the worst of the bunch, have created Stalinist personality cults and ruthlessly suppress all dissent. In Uzbektstan's most recent election, President Karimov ran against an unknown, handpicked opponent who boasted on Election Day that he too had voted for Karimov. Just days before a visit by Powell [in] December [2001] the Uzbek Parliament announced its intention to name Karimov President-for-Life.

Thousands have been arrested in Uzbekistan by the National Security Service (successor to the Uzbek KGB) simply because they questioned government policies or were thought to practice Islam too devoutly. Human Rights Watch claims that police torture has resulted in the deaths of at least 15 Uzbek prisoners in the past two years. Observers say that Uzbekistan's combination of poverty, unemployment and brutal repression is pushing small but increasing numbers of Uzbeks into radical Islamic groups that operate covertly and stand opposed to Karimov's regime.

Bush officials say they are working to promote democracy in the region, and they have spoken out against some human rights violations and various perversions of the democratic process. Yet on January 30 [2002], State Department spokesman Richard Boucher confirmed that Uzbekistan could expect a three-fold increase in foreign aid for the coming year. The Uzbek aid request is not tied to any improvement in the country's human rights record. Although Sen. Paul Wellstone (D-Minnesota) added language to the Foreign Operations Bill requiring the State Department to report on Uzbek human rights, few expect much Senate opposition to the administration's request for increased aid. There's certainly no discussion in Congress of the larger question of whether anyone besides local dictators and oil company executives stand to benefit from America's presence in Central Asia.

Back in Bishkek, Marat and his friends have waited several weeks but still haven't received any job offers from U.S. officials. The pay-off for most other people in Central Asia and the United States may prove equally illusory.

The Small Arms Trade in Afghanistan Is a Threat to Peace

By Ken Silverstein

As the war on terrorism seemed to be winding down in Afghanistan in No-vember and December of 2001, concern arose over the sheer volume of arms that had poured into Afghanistan during twenty years of internal conflict and civil war. Ken Silverstein, a freelance writer based in Washington, D.C., who writes frequently about the post–Cold War arms trade, argues in the follow-ing article that this proliferation of guns is a threat to continued peace in the region. He shows that the disbursement of weapons, from the Soviet invasion of Afghanistan onward, impacted the stability of the region. Silverstein goes on to point out that, given the role of weapons in tipping the balance of po-litical power in Afghanistan's past, the current arms trade must be curtailed to ensure the country's future peace.

E ven as the main fighting in Afghanistan appears to be winding down, a two-decade-long flow of weapons into the country is pick-ing up steam. Starting in October [2001] the United States began drop-ping arms to the so-called Northern Alliance by air, and in recent days the CIA has been funneling assault rifles and other small arms to anti-Taliban fighters who besieged Kandahar. In Congress, a move is afoot to provide direct military assistance to anti-Taliban forces. The Euro-pean Union recently ended a ban on weapons sales to the Northern Al-liance, which is already receiving, at American urging, tanks, armored personnel carriers and infantry fighting vehicles from Russia.

Ken Silverstein, "The Guns of Kabul," *The Nation*, vol. 273, December 31, 2001, pp. 14–18. Copy-right © 2001 by *The Nation*. Reproduced by permission.

Meanwhile, despite being barred from importing weapons by a United Nations embargo, the Taliban were busily rearming their forces until shortly before US planes began bombing Afghanistan on October 7. Its chief suppliers were black-market brokers based in Eastern Europe and private suppliers in Pakistan, who had been shipping the Taliban substantial quantities of assault rifles, rocket launchers and machine guns.

These new shipments come on top of an estimated $8 billion worth of arms that foreign sources have pumped into Afghanistan since the Soviet Union sent troops there in 1979 to prop up a client regime, thereby escalating fighting that has continued uninterrupted to the present day. The CIA, which armed the *mujahedeen* rebels [Islamic Holy warriors] who ultimately forced the withdrawal of the Red Army, supplied much of that weaponry, but at every new stage of warfare a variety of nations have helped refill the arsenals of the competing Afghan factions. During the course of the fighting, 1.5 million Afghans have been killed, a huge chunk of the population has been displaced and the country's economy has been completely destroyed.

Today, Afghanistan is a country divided among heavily armed ethnic factions, and political expression is largely exercised through the barrel of a gun. It is also a place where the laws of supply and demand, combined with corruption and porous borders, have made weapons so easily available that assault rifles can be had for as little as $50. "If I send a truck full of weapons to the [Afghan-Pakistani] border and have $1,000 to hand out, my truck will get through," says an arms dealer with long experience in South Asia. "Osama bin Laden and his friends can do the same thing" (or could have, until a short time ago).

All of this means that establishing anything approaching normal government in post-Taliban Afghanistan is going to be immensely difficult. "There's no chance of a lasting peace unless there's an international presence there that collects most of the arms that are in circulation," says Daniel Nelson, a former Pentagon official and adviser to Congressional leaders. "Every faction in a future government is going to be armed to the teeth and prepared to go back to the mountains if it doesn't get what it wants."

Arming Afghanistan

At the time of the Soviet move into Afghanistan in 1979, the cold war was still going strong. The [U.S.] Carter Administration immediately stepped up what had been a modest program of covert military support for rebels who opposed the pro-Soviet regime. At that time, modern weaponry was not readily available in Afghanistan. John Miley, a retired military officer who helped supply the CIA with arms for the rebels, recalls that when he began procuring matériel, the "weapon of choice" for the typical *mujahedeen* fighter was the Lee Enfield .303, a World War I vintage bolt-action rifle.

That soon changed, particularly after Ronald Reagan took office in 1981 and increased the scope of covert aid. With the help of Saudi Arabia and Pakistan, the CIA set up an elaborate arms pipeline to support the rebels. Among the arms supplied by the agency were some 400,000 Russian assault rifles, Italian antipersonnel mines, Swiss antiaircraft guns, Egyptian mortars, British missiles, Chinese rockets, Indian rifles, Turkish ammunition and American antiaircraft missiles. The CIA even airlifted in pack mules from Tennessee to help transport the arms to the *mujahedeen* over the mountainous terrain. It's estimated that half of all the weapons now floating around Afghanistan were originally sent by the United States and the Soviet Union during the cold war era.

American policy in Afghanistan was focused exclusively on the Soviet Union. However, Pakistan—which was in charge of distributing the weapons to the *mujahedeen*—cared less about Communism than about using the conflict in Afghanistan to strengthen its position vis-à-vis India. It wanted to see a strong Islamic state emerge in Afghanistan and therefore insured that the majority of covert aid supplied through the CIA pipeline went to the most radical rebel groups. The Pakistanis also handled military training and political indoctrination for the rebels. These included large numbers who came from the Middle East, among them the wealthy Saudi Osama bin Laden.

In February of 1989, Mikhail Gorbachev announced the final pullout of Russian troops from Afghanistan, but the Soviets left behind a Communist regime headed by Muhammad Najibullah. Reagan Administration Secretary of State George Shultz proposed that the United States and the Soviets halt all further arms shipments into Afghanistan, a policy he labeled "negative symmetry." Moscow, however, insisted on its right to arm Najibullah and carried out a massive airlift of equipment to its ally. The United States followed suit, and a new spiral of warfare got under way.

Within three years, the various *mujahedeen* factions evicted Najibullah from power. Unfortunately, they almost immediately turned on each other. Armed with stocks captured from the Najibullah government and the vast arsenals acquired from the CIA, the factions—most which now belong to the Northern Alliance—reduced one-third of Kabul to rubble by 1994 in fighting that left 25,000 dead. Outside Kabul, the country was carved up among the various factions, with many *mujahedeen* commanders establishing themselves as warlords. "Even before the Soviet invasion, Afghanistan had a Wild West atmosphere," says Sumit Ganguly, a professor of Asian studies at the University of Texas. "Infusing a society like that with sophisticated weaponry increased the level of lethal violence and helped produce a complete collapse of order."

Disgust with the Northern Alliance paved the way for the rise of the Taliban, which took effective control of the country in 1996. Fighting continued, though, and once again the various warring parties had no trouble getting weapons. The Taliban now inherited the huge cold-war-era stocks—including hundreds of Russian tanks and about seventy-five fighter planes—and supplemented their supplies with the help of Pakistani middlemen buying small arms in Hong Kong and Dubai. They also tapped armories in the former Eastern bloc states, where corrupt military officers and factory managers have created a thriving black market. Before his assassination in a September 9, 2001, suicide bomb attack by two Arabs posing as journalists, Northern Alliance commander Ahmed Shah Massoud charged that the Taliban had received tanks, automatic rifles, mines and bombs from Ukraine. (To pay for the weapons, the Taliban used tens of millions of dollars they raised annually from a tax imposed on drug sales. The Northern Alliance also profited from the drug trade.)

A Burgeoning Arms Trade

The United States walked away from Afghanistan once it achieved its objective of toppling the Communist government there, but Pakistan saw the Taliban as a useful tool and became their most important ally. A Human Rights Watch report from July 2001 says that Pakistan's Inter-Services Intelligence directorate played a key role in "bankrolling Taliban operations . . . arranging training for Taliban fighters . . . planning and directing offensives, providing and facilitating shipments of ammunition and fuel, and on several occasions apparently directly providing combat support." The Saudis also supported the Taliban, whom they saw as a means of increasing their influence in South Asia and countering the influence of Iran, which supported several Shiite factions in the Northern Alliance.

Meanwhile, the Northern Alliance had its own network of outside sponsors. Iran—which opposed the spread of the Taliban's ideology to other areas of the Muslim world as well as greater Saudi influence in the region—was its most important supplier of military hardware. Fearing the spread of Islamic radicalism to the former Soviet republics, Russia also provided substantial direct support to the Northern Alliance and served as the chief conduit for Iranian aid. India, hoping to check Pakistan's moves, offered additional support to anti-Taliban forces, though it played a less important role than Teheran and Moscow.

The end result was that a flood of small arms continued to pour into Afghanistan. Alexander Thier, an officer-in-charge for the United Nations humanitarian office in Afghanistan during the mid-1990s, says that weapons have become so pervasive that they've come to play an important economic role in the country. "Other than drugs or basic foodstuffs, arms and ammunition are about the only items that can be sold or traded," he says. "The only way for young men to get a job is to pick up a gun and join one of the factions." Indeed, Afghanistan is so saturated with arms that it has become what Tara Kartha, an arms specialist at the New Delhi-based Institute for Defense Studies and Analyses, describes as a "weapons warehouse." Arms from Afghanistan have been traced to the guerrilla groups in Chechnya, Uzbekistan and the Philippines. "Weapons are flowing both into and out of Afghanistan," says Michael Klare, professor of peace and world security studies at Hampshire College. "If one of the factions is short on cash, it will sell part of its stocks to buyers outside the country."

One of the scarier legacies of the cold war era is the US-supplied Stinger missiles, which the *mujahedeen* used to great effect against Soviet helicopter gunships. Hundreds were left behind in Afghanistan, and they became something of a cult item on the international black market. In recent years, they have turned up in the United Arab Emirates, Somalia, Iraq, Qatar, Zambia and North Korea, among other places. They are also believed to be in the arsenals of antigovernment guerrillas in Turkey and Sri Lanka, as well as those of Hezbollah in Lebanon. The CIA was so worried about the proliferation of Stingers that in the mid-1990s it allocated $55 million to try to buy them back on the black market. Despite offering up to $200,000 each—about six times the original price—the program has met with virtually no success.

Though the various Afghan parties meeting in Bonn reached an agreement on December 4, 2001, it's hard to be optimistic about what comes next in Afghanistan, given the number of armed parties now competing for power. Mohammed Ayoob, a professor of international relations at Michigan State University, describes the Afghan warlords as "entrepreneurs" who gain political and economic benefits from continued fighting. Those benefits include their control of the drug trade, their ability to run extortion rackets that force civilians to pay for protection and the subsidies they receive from foreign states. "The warlords don't want to see the fighting end," he says.

Patching together a settlement among the foreign nations that have been arming the Afghan fighters may be as complicated as negotiating an internal settlement among the warlords. Pakistan is determined that the Pashtuns win a large role in the post-Taliban government. Russia and Iran are equally determined to prevent such an outcome, though they are split in regard to which factions they want to see in control of the government.

Much of what happens now will depend on the role played by the United States. Among other things, it must take the lead in halting shipments of arms and pressure other parties to do the same. American officials have suggested that only those groups that agree to disarm will be eligible to receive US aid, but there's a big loophole: The factions will be allowed to keep the majority of their small arms—the cause of most of the death and destruction since 1979.

⚜ IMPORTANT FIGURES

Alexander the Great: Conqueror of the Persian Empire; conquered Afghanistan between 330 and 327 B.C.

Osama bin Laden: An exiled Saudi militant, former mujahid, and head of the al-Qaeda terrorist network.

Mohammad Daud: Afghan prime minister who seized power from King Zahir Shah in 1973.

Rashid Dostum: The military leader of the Northern Alliance after the assassination of Ahmad Shah Massoud.

Ahmad Shah Durrani: The Afghan ruler who in 1757 conquered the territory that today constitutes Afghanistan.

Gulbuddin Hekmatyar: The fundamentalist leader of the largest Pashtun mujahideen party (Hezb-e-Islami) that opposed the Soviets; he fought Ahmad Shah Massoud in the 1992–1996 civil war and fled the Taliban in 1996. Hekmatyar returned to Afghanistan after the signing of the Bonn Agreement.

Hamid Karzai: The interim leader of Afghanistan since the fall of the Taliban in December 2001.

Ahmad Shah Massoud: The Northern Alliance commander who was assassinated just days before the September 11, 2001, attacks on the Pentagon and the World Trade Center.

Pervez Musharraf: The president of Pakistan since 2001 (chief executive since 1999).

Burhanuddin Rabbani: The president of Afghanistan from 1992 to 1996, when he was deposed by the Taliban. Thereafter, he served as the political head of the Northern Alliance.

GLOSSARY

Bonn Agreement: The UN-sponsored agreement forming an interim government in Afghanistan, signed in Bonn, Germany.

burka: An all-enveloping, head-to-toe covering (or veil) with a mesh grid over the eyes worn by Afghan women since the Taliban's rule.

hajj: The annual Muslim pilgrimage to Mecca.

haram: "Religiously forbidden."

Hezb-e-Islami: "Party of Islam"; a fundamentalist group led by Gulbuddin Hekmatyar, the former darling of Pakistani militarist circles.

ISI: Inter-Services Intelligence, Pakistan's secret police.

Islam: One of the world's major religions. *Islam* is an Arabic term that means "submission"—in this case to the will of God (Allah).

Jamaat-e-Islami: "Society of Islam"; a Pakistani party led by Qazi Hussain Ahmad, the main fundamentalist supporter of Gulbuddin Hekmatyar and some other fundamentalist groups in Afghanistan.

Jamiat-e-Islami: "Society of Islam"; the biggest fundamentalist group in Afghanistan, led by Burhanuddin Rabbani.

jihad: A holy war to defend Islam; also, the struggle to become a good Muslim.

jihadi: One who participates in jihad (Islamic holy war).

Khalq and Parcham: "The People" and "The Banner"; factions of the pro-Soviet People's Democratic Party of Afghanistan (PDPA), which was installed in power through a bloody coup on April 27, 1978. It was overthrown by fundamentalists on April 28, 1992.

Koran (or Quran): The Islamic book of holy scriptures, written by the prophet Muhammad based on revelations received from Allah.

Loya Jirga: Grand council; a traditional meeting of all tribal elders to resolve large-scale problems.

madrassas: Islamic religious schools in Pakistan that are thought to be the breeding ground of the Taliban movement.

mujahideen: Islamic holy warriors/freedom fighters.

mullah: A highly placed Islamic religious leader.

NGO: Nongovernmental organization.

Northern Alliance (or United Front): A military alliance composed of some jihadi fundamentalist groups and former mujahideen, mostly non-Pashtuns.

Pashtun: A member of Afghanistan's largest ethnic group, concentrated mostly in the southern part of the country.

PDPA: See *Khalq and Parchan.*

al-Qaeda: "The Base" in Arabic; a global terrorist network founded and headed by Osama bin Laden.

Ramadan: The ninth month of the Muslim lunar calendar, a holy month of fasting.

shalwar kameez: The baggy pants and long shirt worn by Afghan men and women.

Sharia (or Shariat): Islamic law.

Shura: The Islamic religious or political council.

Taliban: An Afghan fundamentalist force believed to be supported heavily by Pakistan. The Taliban ruled Afghanistan from 1996 to 2001.

ulema: Islamic scholars.

Wahhabi: An extremist sect of Islam that began in Saudi Arabia.

♦ CHRONOLOGY

B.C.

330–327
Alexander the Great conquers Afghanistan.

A.D.

699–700
Arabs conquer Afghanistan and introduce Islam to the region.

1155–1227
Genghis Khan's army marches across Asia. Afghanistan becomes a part of his dominion.

1809
England signs a treaty of mutual defense with the ruler of Afghanistan against Russia and France.

1839–1842
The First Anglo-Afghan War occurs.

1878–1880
The Second Anglo-Afghan War occurs. England is placed in charge of Afghan foreign affairs as a result of the Treaty of Gandamak.

1880–1901
The boundaries of the modern Afghan state are determined through a series of international agreements.

1919–1929
Afghanistan regains its independence after a third war against the British army. The 1919 Treaty of Rawalpindi makes Afghanistan free to conduct its own foreign affairs. King Amanullah attempts to institute a reform movement to modernize the nation, but it meets severe resistance from religious leadership.

1929
Amanullah is forced to flee due to civil unrest regarding his reforms.

1933–1973
Zahir Shah becomes king, and Afghanistan remains a monarchy for the next four decades.

1953
General Mohammad Daud becomes prime minister; he turns to the Soviet Union for economic and military assistance.

1973
Mohammad Daud seizes power in a military coup and declares Afghanistan a republic.

1978
The People's Democratic Party of Afghanistan (PDPA), a Communist organization, takes power through a military coup.

1979
The Soviet army invades Afghanistan.

1988
Afghanistan, the Soviet Union, the United States, and Pakistan sign peace accords, and the Soviet Union begins pulling out troops.

1989
The last Soviet troops leave, but civil war between the Afghan government and tribal warlords continues.

1991
The United States and Soviet Union agree to end military aid to both sides.

1992
Tribal warlords close in on Kabul and the government collapses. They then battle for control of the country.

1992–1996
Civil war between heavily armed tribal militias continues to tear the country apart.

1996
The Taliban seizes control of Kabul and imposes a fundamentalist version of Islam on Afghanistan.

1998
The United States launches Tomahawk missiles at suspected bases of

militant Osama bin Laden, who is accused of bombing U.S. embassies in Africa.

2001

March: The Taliban destroys giant Buddha statues despite international efforts to save them.

May: The Taliban orders religious minorities to wear tags identifying themselves as non-Muslims and orders Hindu women to veil themselves like other Afghan women.

September 9: Ahmad Shah Massoud, legendary guerrilla and leader of the main opposition to the Taliban, is killed, apparently by assassins posing as journalists.

September 11: The World Trade Center in New York City and the Pentagon in Washington, D.C., are attacked. Osama bin Laden, guest of the Taliban and founder of the al-Qaeda terrorist network, is held responsible by the U.S. government for the attacks.

October: The United States and Britain launch air strikes against Afghanistan after the Taliban refuses to hand over bin Laden.

November: Coalition forces seize Kabul and other key cities.

December: U.S.-led forces launch a bombing campaign against the Tora Bora cave complex in southeastern Afghanistan in an effort to crush Taliban and al-Qaeda forces hiding there.

December 5: Afghan groups sign an agreement in Bonn, Germany, forming an interim government.

December 7: The Taliban gives up the southern city of Kandahar, but Taliban leader Mullah Omar remains at large.

December 22: Hamid Karzai, an ethnic Pashtun, is sworn in as the head of a thirty-member interim power-sharing government.

2002

March: U.S.-led forces launch Operation Anaconda in an attempt to destroy remnants of the Taliban and al-Qaeda.

April 18: Former king Zahir Shah returns, but says he makes no claim on the throne.

May: Allied forces continue their military campaign to find remnants of al-Qaeda and Taliban forces in the southeast.

June 11: Loya Jirga (the grand council) opens.

June 13: Loya Jirga elects Hamid Karzai as interim head of state. Karzai picks members of his administration, which is to serve until 2004.

July: Vice President Haji Abdul Qadir is assassinated by gunmen in Kabul. A U.S. air raid in the Uruzgan province kills forty-eight civilians, many of them members of a wedding party.

September: Karzai narrowly escapes an assassination attempt in Kandahar, his hometown. As a result, he replaces his Afghan bodyguards with U.S. special forces.

October: The top United Nations envoy in Afghanistan tells the UN Security Council that the new Afghan government headed by Karzai does not have the power to deal with the underlying problems that cause security threats in the nation.

November: Rival factions in northern Afghanistan begin turning in their weapons as part of a UN program to curb violence. Former king Zahir Shah inaugurates a special committee to draft a new constitution for Afghanistan.

December: Afghan commander Amanullah Khan launches an attack on positions held by Ismail Khan, governor of the Herat province.

2003

January: The Afghan security chief claims that minor clashes have been reported between Afghan forces and suspected members of the Taliban. President Karzai announces the formation of four commissions to accelerate the disarmament of warlord armies and to rebuild the Afghan National Army.

February: President Karzai visits the U.S. Senate Foreign Relations Committee in Washington, D.C. In the hearing, Karzai gives an optimistic view of the state of Afghanistan and disputes claims that one hundred thousand militiamen living in the provinces are beyond the control of his government. Factional fighting flares up between rival Afghan groups within seven hundred yards of the perimeter of Bagram air base.

March: Afghan authorities raid a house in Kandahar and arrest ten members of the former Taliban regime. Police seize arms, explosives, and land mines. The first Afghan radio station programmed solely for women begins broadcasting in Kabul.

April: Officials announce a UN program to disarm, demobilize, and reintegrate an estimated one hundred thousand fighters across Afghanistan in the next three years. Nearly fifty suspected Taliban fighters attack a checkpoint in the Shingai district of Zabul province; the fighters flee after a brief gun battle.

May: Afghanistan's membership in the International Criminal Court (ICC) takes effect. The ICC will have the authority to investigate and prosecute serious war crimes and crimes against humanity committed on Afghan soil.

2004

June: The first free elections are scheduled to take place in Afghanistan.

❧ FOR FURTHER RESEARCH

Books

S.H. Amin, *Law, Reform, and Revolution in Afghanistan: Implications for Central Asia and the Islamic World.* Glasgow, Scotland: Royston, 1993.

George Arney, *Afghanistan.* London: Mandarin, 1990.

Anthony Arnold, *The Fateful Pebble: Afghanistan's Role in the Fall of the Soviet Empire.* Novato, CA: Presidio Press, 1993.

Gary K. Bertsch, Cassady B. Craft, and Scott A. Jones, eds., *Crossroads and Conflict: Security and Foreign Policy in the Caucasus and Central Asia.* New York: Routledge, 1999.

Yossef Bodansky, *Bin Laden: The Man Who Declared War on America.* Rocklin, CA: Prima, 1999.

Artem Borovik, *The Hidden War: A Russian Journalist's Account of the Soviet War in Afghanistan.* New York: Atlantic Monthly Press, 1990.

Henry S. Bradsher, *Afghan Communism and Soviet Intervention.* Oxford, England: Oxford University Press, 1999.

John K. Cooley, *Unholy Wars: Afghanistan, American, and International Terrorism.* London and Sterling, VA: Pluto Press, 2000.

Diego Cordovez, *Out of Afghanistan: The Inside Story of the Soviet Withdrawal.* New York: Oxford University Press, 1995.

Helene Carrere d'Encausse, *Islam and the Russian Empire: Reform and Revolution in Central Asia.* Trans. Quintin Hoare. Berkeley and Los Angeles: University of California Press, 1989.

Shams Ud Din, *Soviet Afghan Relations.* Calcutta, India: K.P. Bagchi, 1985.

David B. Edwards, *Heroes of the Age: Moral Fault Lines on the Afghan Frontier.* Berkeley and Los Angeles: University of California Press, 1996.

Anoushiravan Ehteshami, *From the Gulf to Central Asia: Players in the New Great Game.* Exeter, England: University of Exeter Press, 1995.

Martin Ewans, *Afghanistan: A New History*. Surrey, England: Curzon Press, 2001.

William K. Fraser, *Afghanistan: A Study of Political Developments in Central and Southern Asia*. New York: AMS Press, 1981.

Mark Galeotti, *Afghanistan: The Soviet Union's Last War*. London: Frank Cass, 1995.

Abdul Ghani, *A Brief Political History of Afghanistan*. Lahore, Pakistan: Najaf, 1989.

Mir Gholam Mohammad Ghobar, *Afghanistan in the Course of History*. Vol. 2. Trans. Sherief A. Fayez. Alexandria, VA: Hashmat K. Gobar, 2001.

M.J. Gohari, *Taliban: Ascent to Power*. Oxford, England: Oxford University Press, 2001.

Larry P. Goodson, *Afghanistan's Endless War: State Failure, Regional Politics, and the Rise of the Taliban*. Seattle: University of Washington Press, 2001.

Michael Griffin, *Reaping the Whirlwind: The Taliban Movement in Afghanistan*. London: Pluto Press, 2001.

Peter Hopkirk, *The Great Game: The Struggle for Empire in Central Asia*. New York: Kodansha America, 1994.

David C. Isby, *War in a Distant Country: Afghanistan, Invasion, and Resistance*. London: Arms and Armour Press, 1989.

Ali Ahmad Jalali and Lester W. Grau, *Afghan Guerrilla Warfare: In the Words of the Mujahideen Fighters*. St. Paul, MN: MBI, 2001.

Hassan Kakar, *Afghanistan: The Soviet Invasion and the Afghan Response, 1979–1982*. Berkeley and Los Angeles: University of California Press, 1995.

Ralph Magnus and Eden Naby, *Afghanistan, Mullah, Marx, and Mujahid*. Boulder, CO: Westview, 1998.

William Maley, ed., *Fundamentalism Reborn? Afghanistan and the Taliban*. New York: New York University Press, 1998.

Peter Marsden, *The Taliban: War and Religion in Afghanistan*. London: Zed Books, 2002.

Kamal Matinnudin, *The Taliban Phenomenon: Afghanistan, 1994–1997*. Oxford, England: Oxford University Press, 1999.

Karl E. Meyer and Shareen Blair Brysac, *Tournament of Shadows: The Great Game and the Race for Empire in Central Asia.* Washington, DC: Counterpoint Press, 1999.

Neamatollah Nojumi, *The Rise of the Taliban in Afghanistan: Mass Mobilization, Civil War, and the Future of the Region.* New York: Palgrave, 2002.

Asta Olsen, *Islam and Politics in Afghanistan.* London: Curzon Press, 1995.

Rasul Bakhsh Rais, *War Without Winners: Afghanistan's Uncertain Transition After the Cold War.* Oxford, England, and Karachi, Pakistan: Oxford University Press, 1994.

Ahmed Rashid, *Jihad: The Rise of Militant Islam in Central Asia.* New York: Penguin Books, 2002.

———, *Taliban: Militant Islam, Oil, and Fundamentalism in Central Asia.* New Haven, CT: Yale University Press, 1998.

Olivier Roy, *Afghanistan: From Holy War to Civil War.* Princeton, NJ: Princeton University Press, 1995.

———, *Islam and Resistance in Afghanistan.* Cambridge, England: Cambridge University Press, 1986.

———, *The New Central Asia: The Creation of Nations.* New York: New York University Press, 2000.

Barnett Rubin, *The Fragmentation of Afghanistan: State Formation and Collapse in the International System.* New Haven, CT: Yale University Press, 1995.

———, *The Search for Peace in Afghanistan: From Buffer State to Failed State.* New Haven, CT: Yale University Press, 1995.

M. Holt Ruffin, Daniel C. Waugh, and S. Frederick Starr, eds., *Civil Society in Central Asia.* Seattle: University of Washington Press, 1999.

Boris Z. Rumer, *Central Asia and the New Global Economy.* Armonk, NY: M.E. Sharpe, 2000.

Russian General Staff, *The Soviet-Afghan War: How a Superpower Fought and Lost.* Trans. and ed. Lester W. Grau and Michal A. Gress. Lawrence: University Press of Kansas, 2002.

Roald Sagdeev and Susan Eisenhower, eds., *Islam and Central Asia: An Enduring Legacy or an Evolving Threat?* New York: Center for Political Studies, 2000.

Rosemarie Skaine, *The Women of Afghanistan Under the Taliban.* Jefferson, NC: McFarland, 2001.

Stephen Tanner, *Afghanistan: A Military History from Alexander the Great to the Fall of the Taliban.* New York: Da Capo Press, 2002.

Richard Tapper, *The Conflict of Tribe and State in Afghanistan.* London: Croom Helm, 1983.

Mark Urban, *War in Afghanistan.* New York: St. Martin's Press, 1988.

Alexei Vassiliev, *Central Asia: Political and Economic Challenges in the Post-Soviet Era.* Beirut and London: Saqi Books, 2001.

K. Warikoo, *Afghanistan Factor in Central and South Asian Politics.* New Delhi, India: Trans Asian Informatics, 1994.

Oleg Yermakov, *Afghan Tales: Stories from Russia's Vietnam.* New York: William Morrow, 1993.

Periodicals

Benazir Bhutto, "Pakistan's Dilemma," *Harvard International Review*, Spring 2002.

Bruce Crumley et al., "Hate Club," *Time*, November 12, 2001.

Laura Flanders, "Afghan Feminists Speak Out," *Progressive*, November 2001.

Carlotta Gall, "Expecting Taliban, but Finding Only Horror," *New York Times*, July 8, 2002.

Michael Ignatieff, "Nation-Building Lite," *New York Times Magazine*, July 28, 2002.

Frederick W. Kagan, "Did We Fail in Afghanistan?" *Commentary*, March 2003.

Elie D. Krakowski, "How to Win the Peace in Afghanistan," *Weekly Standard*, July 8, 2002.

Rose V. Lindgren, "When Foreign Intervention Is Justified: Women Under the Taliban," *Humanist*, July/August 2002.

Michael Massing, "Losing the Peace?" *Nation*, May 13, 2002.

Tim McGirk, "Al-Qaeda's New Hideouts," *Time*, July 29, 2002.

Rod Nordland, Sami Yousafzai, and Babak Dehghanpishheh, "How al-Qaeda Slipped Away," *Newsweek*, August 19, 2002.

Olivier Roy, "Why War Is Going On in Afghanistan: The Afghan Crisis in Perspective," *Journal of International Affairs*, December 2000–February 2001.

Horst Rutsch, "Afghanistan: On the Road to Recovery," *UN Chronicle*, March–May 2002.

Philip Smucker, "Afghans Put Off Key Decisions," *Christian Science Monitor*, June 18, 2002.

Raymond Whittaker, "Behind the Burqa: Women Who Fight the Taliban," *In These Times*, November 12, 2001.

Websites

About Afghanistan, www.aboutafghanistan.com. This search engine directs researchers to a wide variety of resources on the web that track topics related to Afghanistan.

Afghan Online Press, www.aopnews.com. This website is a media center for current events in Afghanistan that combines radio and television news broadcasts with printed articles in a variety of languages.

Human Rights Watch: Afghanistan, www.hrw.org. Human Rights Watch is an independent, nongovernmental organization dedicated to protecting the human rights of people around the world.

The Reconstruction of Afghanistan, www.developmentgateway.org. The Development Gateway is an interactive portal for information and knowledge sharing on sustainable development and poverty reduction. This site is dedicated to the reconstruction of Afghanistan.

The Revolutionary Association of the Women of Afghanistan, www. rawa.org. RAWA, the Revolutionary Association of the Women of Afghanistan, was established in Kabul, Afghanistan, in 1977 as an independent political/social organization of Afghan women fighting for human rights and for social justice in Afghanistan. This site tracks Afghan developments from a social justice perspective.

🔥 INDEX